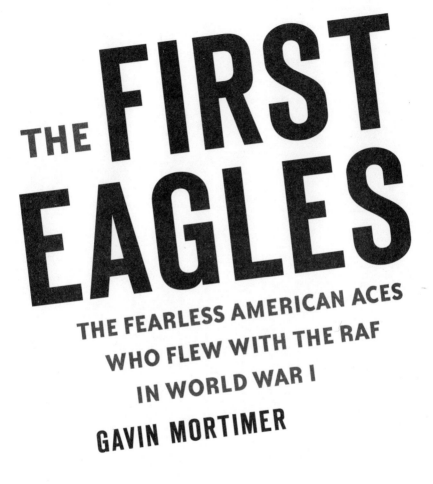

THE FIRST EAGLES

THE FEARLESS AMERICAN ACES
WHO FLEW WITH THE RAF
IN WORLD WAR I

GAVIN MORTIMER

ZENITH PRESS

But ye who fearless flew to meet the foe,
Eagles of freedom,—nevermore, we know,
Shall we behold you floating far away.
Yet clouds and birds and every starry ray
Will draw our hearts to where your spirits glow
In the blue heaven.

—**"In the Blue Heaven," Henry van Dyke, 1919**

First published in 2014 by Zenith Press, an imprint of Quarto Publishing Group USA Inc., 400 First Avenue North, Suite 400, Minneapolis, MN 55401 USA

© 2014 Quarto Publishing Group USA Inc.
Text © 2014 Gavin Mortimer

Zenith Press titles are also available at discounts in bulk quantity for industrial or sales-promotional use. For details write to Special Sales Manager at Quarto Publishing Group USA Inc., 400 First Avenue North, Suite 400, Minneapolis, MN 55401 USA.

To find out more about our books, visit us online at www.zenithpress.com.

ISBN-13: 978-0-7603-4639-6

Library of Congress Cataloging-in-Publication Data

Mortimer, Gavin.
  The first eagles : the fearless American aces who flew with the RAF in World War I / Gavin Mortimer.
     pages cm
  Includes bibliographical references.
  ISBN 978-0-7603-4639-6 (hc w/jacket)
  1. World War, 1914-1918--Aerial operations, American. 2. World War, 1914-1918--Aerial operations, British. 3. Fighter pilots--United States--Biography. 4. Great Britain. Royal Air Force--History--World War, 1914-1918. 5. Americans--Great Britain--History--20th century. I. Title.
  D606.M67 2014
  940.4'4841092313--dc23
                              2014004703

Aquiring Editor: Erik Gilg
Project Manager: Madeleine Vasaly
Design Manager: James Kegley
Cover Designer: Andrew Brozyna
Layout: Helena Shimizu
Map Designer: Philip Schwartzberg

Printed in the United States of America

10 9 8 7 6 5 4 3 2 1

CONTENTS

The Flyers

Name	Date and Place of Birth	Training and Shipment	Service
Alvin Callender	1893, New Orleans, Louisiana.	Trained in Canada and shipped out to England February 1918.	32 Squadron RAF
Laurence Callahan	1895, Louisville, Kentucky.	Trained USA and shipped out to England on SS *Carmania*, September 1917.	85 Squadron RAF and 148th Aero
Frank Dixon	1896, California.	Trained USA and shipped out to England on SS *Carmania*, September 1917.	209 Squadron RAF and 17th Aero
John Donaldson	1897, Fort Yates, North Dakota.	Trained in Canada and shipped out to England May 1918.	32 Squadron RAF
John McGavock Grider	1892, Sans Souci, Arkansas.	Trained USA and shipped out to England on SS *Carmania*, September 1917.	85 Squadron RAF
Frank Hale	1895, Syracuse, New York.	Trained in Canada and shipped out to England May 1918.	32 Squadron RAF
Lloyd Hamilton	1894, Troy, New York.	Trained USA and shipped out to England on SS *Carmania*, September 1917.	3 Squadron RAF and 17th Aero

Name	Date and Place of Birth	Training and Shipment	Service
Reed Landis	1896, Ottawa, Illinois.	Trained USA and shipped out to England on RMS *Aurania*, August 1917.	40 Squadron RAF and 25th Aero
Jens Larson	1891, Boston, Massachusetts.	Enlisted in the RFC 1916 and trained in England.	8, 34, and 84 Squadrons RAF
Oliver LeBoutillier	1895, Montclair, New Jersey.	Trained in New York, shipped out from Canada fall 1916.	209 Squadron RAF
Fred Libby	1892, Sterling, Colorado.	Enlisted in the Canadian army 1914 and volunteered for the RFC 1916.	11, 22, and 25 Squadrons RFC
Bennett Oliver	1895, Pittsburgh, Pennsylvania.	Trained USA and shipped out to England on RMS *Aurania*, August 1917.	84 Squadron RAF and 148th Aero
Donald Poler	1896, Medina, New York.	Trained USA and shipped out to England on SS *Carmania*, September 1917.	40 Squadron RAF and 25th Pursuit
Orville Ralston	1894, Weeping Water, Nebraska.	Trained in Canada and shipped out to England 1918.	85 Squadron and 148th Aero
Bogart Rogers	1897, Los Angeles, California.	Trained in Canada and shipped out to England February 1918.	32 Squadron, RAF
Elliot White Springs	1896, Lancaster, South Carolina.	Trained USA and shipped out to England on SS *Carmania*, September 1917.	85 Squadron and 148th Aero
Arthur Taber	1893, Long Island, New York.	Trained USA and shipped out to England on SS *Carmania*, September 1917.	Aviation Section, Signal Reserve Corps
George Vaughn	1897, Brooklyn, New York.	Trained USA and shipped out to England on SS *Carmania*, September 1917.	84 Squadron RAF and 17th Aero

RFC/RAF Flight Schools in Great Britain

Scotland

Aberdeen

Glasgow   Edinburgh

⊗ Ayr
⊗ Turnberry

North Sea

Carlisle   Newcastle

Belfast

⊗ Redcar

UNITED

Lancaster

Irish Sea

Leeds   Hull

Manchester
⊗ Liverpool   Sheffield

Dublin   Lincoln

KINGDOM

⊗ Grantham

Leicester   ⊗ Stamford
Peterborough   Norwich

Birmingham   Coventry

Wales

Cambridge

England

⊗ Oxford
⊗ London Colney

Houslow ⊗   London

Bristol

Dover ⊗

Romsey ⊗   Calais
Southampton

FRANCE

Plymouth

English Channel

0   50   100 miles

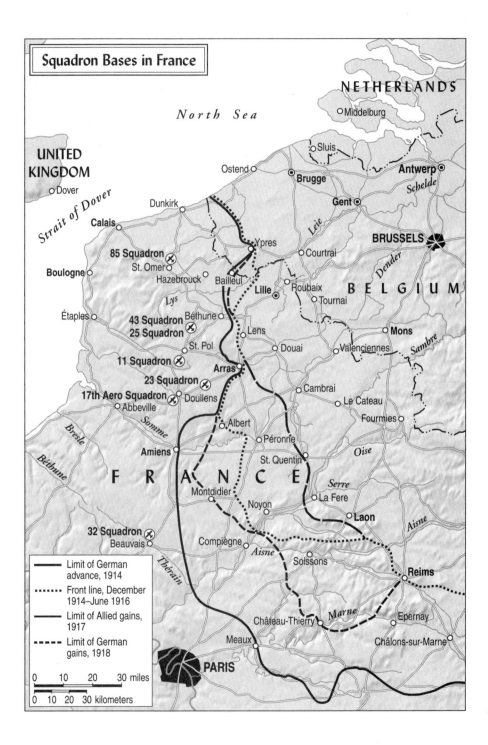

Squadron Bases in France

NETHERLANDS

North Sea

○ Middelburg

UNITED
KINGDOM

○ Dover

Strait of Dover

○ Sluis

Ostend ○

● **Brugge**

Antwerp ◉

Schelde

Dunkirk ○

Gent ◉

Calais ○

Boulogne ○

85 Squadron ⊗
St. Omer ○

Hazebrouck ○   Bailleul ○

Ypres ○

○ Courtrai

BRUSSELS ✷

Dender

Lille ◉   Roubaix ○

○ Tournai

B E L G I U M

Étaples ○

Lys

43 Squadron ⊗
25 Squadron ⊗   Béthune ○

St. Pol ○

Lens ○

Douai ○

Valenciennes ○

Mons ●

Sambre

11 Squadron ⊗

23 Squadron ⊗

Arras ○

Cambrai ○

○ Le Cateau

17th Aero Squadron ⊗   Doullens ○
○ Abbeville

Somme

Albert ○

Fourmies ○

Bresle

Péronne ○

Oise

Béthune

Amiens ●

St. Quentin ○

F R   A   **N**   C   **E**

Montdidier ○

Serre

Noyon ○   La Fère ○

Laon ◉

32 Squadron ⊗
Beauvais ○

Compiègne ○

Aisne

Aisne

Soissons ○

Aisne

Reims ◉

	Limit of German advance, 1914
	Front line, December 1914–June 1916
	Limit of Allied gains, 1917
	Limit of German gains, 1918

Thérain

Marne

Château-Thierry ○

Epernay ○

Meaux ○

Châlons-sur-Marne ○

PARIS ✷

0   10   20   30 miles

0   10   20   30 kilometers

INTRODUCTION

A Useless Fad

On the penultimate day of December 1911, two young men greeted each other warmly in the dining room of New York's Plaza Hotel. They were debonair, assured, their words and mannerisms those of men who had made their mark in the world. With them was a reporter from the *World* newspaper.

One of the men, Walter Brookins, was American, a native of Ohio and the first pilot to be trained by the Wright brothers. The previous year he had soared to an unprecedented height of 4,380 feet. His dining companion was Claude Grahame-White, a dashing Englishman with a touch of the dandy about him. He was a celebrity as much as an aviator and, in 1910, had taken the United States by storm winning the International Aviation Cup at New York's Belmont Park and also scooping a $10,000 first prize in a race from the park to the Statue of Liberty and back.

Grahame-White was back in Manhattan visiting friends and the *World* wanted to hear both his and Brookins's views on the future of aviation. The conservative American was of the opinion that this new mode of transport still had a long way to go; his eyes nearly popped out of their head when the radical Englishman in turn declared over his first course that he would "make a bet with anyone that in twenty years' time we will be flying across the Atlantic Ocean in fifteen hours."

The discussion turned to military aviation, and again Brookins erred on the side of caution. The German Zeppelin dirigible was, he said ominously, a most "dreadful weapon" that could revolutionize

Claude Grahame-White was not only a pioneer pilot; he was also an aviation visionary. *Library of Congress*

warfare. Grahame-White snorted dismissively. Why, the dirigible was obsolescent! No, the future was the airplane, said Grahame-White, adding as he reached for his glass, "I have made it a rule of late to avoid speaking about the uses of the airplane to avoid being laughed at." The reporter asked why people laughed at him. "People don't realize the importance of this branch of the military service," replied the Englishman. "It is enough to say that the airplane's field in military and naval work is unlimited."

Some of those who laughed at Grahame-White were military men. Britain's chief of the Imperial general staff in 1910, William Nicholson, derided the airplane as "a useless and expensive fad," a view shared by Rear Adm. Robley D. Evans, erstwhile commander of the "Great White Fleet," the popular name bestowed upon the U.S. Navy battle fleet that circumnavigated the globe from 1907 to 1909 on the orders of President Theodore Roosevelt. Evans was widely quoted in newspapers in September 1910, declaring that "flying machines have plenty of work ahead of them before navy men will consider them a serious menace." Evans was speaking shortly after Congress had refused to fund research into the use of the airplane as a weapon of war. Evans agreed with his political masters, rubbishing suggestions an airplane could ever sink a battleship. "It is only necessary to state that our service revolvers are deadly weapons at a range of 300 feet and that several hundred experts on each ship would be using them in earnest."

Rear Admiral Robley D. Evans (left) of the U.S. Navy was skeptical that aircraft would ever pose a threat to battleships. *Library of Congress*

Evans commanded the "Great White Fleet," the popular name bestowed upon the U.S. Navy battle fleet that circumnavigated the globe from 1907 to 1909. *Library of Congress*

Writing in the September 1910 issue of *Popular Mechanics*, Capt. Richmond P. Hobson, a naval man who had resigned his commission in 1907 to become Democratic representative from Alabama, said "the offensive power of the airplane . . . is almost negligible." This view was challenged in the December issue of the journal by noted engineer Victor Lougheed, whose younger brothers, Allan and Malcom, would later form the Lockheed Aircraft Company. Far from the airplane having a negligible impact in war, Lougheed believed it was the battleship that was obsolescent, writing: "They must surely take their final place with the other extravagances and follies of progressing mankind with such other colossal extravagances of human efforts as the pyramids—like them wonders of a world, but regarded as such more because of their uselessness and worthlessness than of such downright efficiency and effectiveness as pertains to the irresistible advance of the inexpensive, developing and wonderfully promising vehicles of the sky."

Lougheed finished his essay with a grave warning for the U.S. government and military: "To assume that the 'offensive power of the airplane . . . is almost negligible' is to court an obsession with the present status that will defeat even a most moderate insight into the future. All the probabilities are that the offensive power of the airplane of the future, and even of the present, is as much underrated as the defensive and offensive power of the battleship against aerial craft is overrated."

Nonetheless, the faith of the U.S. military in the airplane eroded still further in 1913 during the Mexican War. The ten Curtiss biplanes sent to the region didn't perform well and "proved more of a liability than a help, breaking down, having forced landings and diverting soldiers and cavalry on the ground from their traditional tasks to aid the stranded pilots."[1]

Sensing a major conflagration was about to erupt in Europe, Congress felt obligated in July 1914 to pass an Act to create the Aviation Section of the Signal Corps, but it was a desultory measure, and the unit's strength was set at sixty officers and 260 enlisted men. To train this ancillary of a subordinate branch, the government grudgingly permitted only the smallest of grants, and when war broke out in Europe on August 3, 1914, the Aviation Section had just five aircraft.

[1] Alan Clark, *Aces High*

Fortunately for the British, at least, their military wasn't staffed entirely by men whose views were firmly entrenched in the past. Among those with foresight were Douglas Haig, chief of the general staff in India, and Lord Horatio Kitchener, appointed secretary of state for war in summer 1914.

One of Kitchener's first acts was to order the nascent Royal Flying Corps (RFC), formed in 1912, to raise five more squadrons. Hugh Trenchard, officer commanding the military wing of the Royal Flying Corps—the man tasked with overseeing the expansion—was delighted, but he was also daunted. Creating five squadrons was a monumental challenge in a country where those who had even clapped eyes on an airplane were in the minority.

An early recruitment poster encouraging young Americans to enlist in the Aviation Section of the Signal Corps. *Library of Congress*

In late August 1914, Maj. Gen. Sir Sam Hughes, Canadian minister of militia and defense, suggested to Trenchard that North America might offer a fertile recruiting ground. After all, the United States was the birthplace of the airplane and there were many hundreds of aviation enthusiasts.

Lord Kitchener was open to the recruitment of pilots to the RFC from Canada but rejected the idea of enlisting Americans. But neither he, nor anyone in the British military, envisaged the extent of the carnage in the world's first truly technological conflict. Between July and December 1916, the RFC lost 499 of its aircrew, with a further 250 incapacitated through physical or psychological wounds. Machines could be replaced—and by late 1916 "a rapidly expanding labor force had already reached 60,000 engaged in the manufacture of airplanes and another 20,000 in building aircraft engines"[2]—but

[2] Ralph Barker, *The Royal Flying Corps in France*

The Germans also used artwork in their quest for aircrew. *Library of Congress*

finding the men to fly them was more of a challenge. Throughout 1916, scores of young men, many fresh out of school, were posted to combat squadrons in France undertrained and ill-equipped to take on the German air force. Most were shot out of the sky within days.

In August 1916, as losses began to mount, the RFC began actively recruiting in Canada, placing advertisements in newspapers calling on men to "Enlist as an Air Pilot." All tuition was free, the ads trumpeted, and from the date of enlistment, trainee aviators would receive $1.10 per day with 25¢ per day flying allowance. Provided prospective enlistees were between eighteen and twenty-five and possessed of a "good moral character with such an education and upbringing as would fit them for positions as officers," they could be granted a commission at the end of a three-month course.

Early in 1917 the British finally turned to the United States. Lieutenant Colonel C. G. Hoare, the commanding officer of the RFC in Canada, persuaded the American military to allow him to visit cities including Chicago, Boston, St. Louis, and Minneapolis in search of manpower, while the British also opened a permanent recruiting mission at 280 Broadway, New York City. Within a short space of time Hoare had drafted in four more officers to deal with the demand. On June 9, 1917, the *New York Times* reported that the previous day, one hundred young men of "sound physique" and "considerable experience with machinery" had been accepted into the RFC. The paper described the recruits as "British and Canadian subjects," which was hogwash, as the journalists well knew. The vast majority were young Americans "tired of waiting for their own country to take her place with the Allies."[3] They were willing to trade nationalities for a time if it meant the chance of seeing some adventure.

Americans had been made aware of the exploits of the RFC thanks to the efforts of anti-isolationist newspapers. In June 1916 the *Connersville Evening News* told its readers in Indiana of Britain's "Birdmen Heroes," glamorizing the RFC with tales of "unbelievable" skill and pluck in the skies over France. The following month the *New York Tribune* syndicated a feature to numerous regional papers that was pure propaganda for the British military. "Looping the Loop Over London" was the heading of the full-page article, which was accompanied by three photographs of England's newest warplane and a breathless account of a trip over London by the *Tribune's* Jane Anderson.[4]

Describing the thrill of "looping the loop" over London's Hyde Park at seven thousand feet, an enraptured Anderson told her

---

[3] John H. Morrow and Earl Rogers, eds., *A Yankee Ace in the RAF*

[4] Ironically, the Atlanta-born Anderson became a fascist during her time living in Spain in the 1920s. During World War II, she broadcast Nazi propaganda on the radio from Germany under the *nom de guerre* "the Georgia Peach." Anderson was arrested after the war and charged with treason, but the indictment was dropped, primarily because in 1934 she had become a Spanish citizen through marriage.

Illinois native Pat O'Brien initially joined the Aviation Section of the U.S. Signal Corps but, frustrated by the lack of action, he crossed to Canada and joined the RFC. After being shot down, O'Brien escaped and wrote a best-selling book about his experiences.

audience: "We circled toward the aerodrome. We dropped down, spiraling . . . the final evidence of the superb construction of his majesty's biplane, designed for the destruction of enemy aircraft. I had full opportunity of discovering whatever weakness or fallibility might have been in her. There was none."

The British were delighted at Anderson's puffery. What propaganda! What better way to sell the RFC to Americans than a stirring account of their very latest warplane? And so it proved, as dozens of restless young Americans, unable to resist the temptation of taking to the skies in combat, crossed the border into Canada and offered their services to the RFC. The volunteers received a medical examination and, once given a clean bill of health, were sent east to Camp Borden, Toronto.

Borden was surrounded by lakes—Huron to the north, Ontario to the south, and Simcoe to the east—but the thousand acres given the RFC by Canada's Department of Militia and Defense were ideal for the business of flying.

Construction on transforming the area into an air base began in January 1917 with 1,700 laborers working furiously to level out the sandy soil, sew it with grass seed, and install "an excellent road system, a first rate water supply and electrical system . . . together with special telephone communications to Toronto and neighboring towns." In time there would also emerge from the prairie a one-hundred-by-forty-foot swimming pool, tennis courts, and nine hole golf course, making it "the finest flying camp in North America."[5]

---

[5] Alan Sullivan, *Aviation in Canada, 1917–1918*

Pat O'Brien flew with 66 Squadron, as did another American, Howard Boysen, seen here on the left.

Working by arc lamps throughout the night, often in temperatures as low as twenty-five degrees below zero, the laborers finished Borden so quickly that training could begin by April 1917. Three months later, the *Boston Globe* reported that Lt. Allan Thomas, a British combat veteran, had opened a recruiting office in the city and was inviting young men to present themselves for an interview and medical examination between the hours of 8:00 a.m. and 5:00 p.m. "He hopes to send at least 200 within the next few weeks to Camp

Borden near Toronto," explained the *Globe*. "At Camp Borden there are 120 airplanes for men to learn to fly with and almost daily as many as 50 machines are in the air at the same time." Thomas was confident that the city of Boston would provide the RFC with more cadets than New York. On the day the correspondent from the *Globe* visited the recruiting office, four Americans passed muster and were dispatched to Canada, each dreaming of earning that most treasured of aviation titles—"ace."

CHAPTER 1

I'm Going to Tell
Them I Raised Hell

George Vaughn came from Brooklyn—from the Washington Avenue area, to be exact. Born in May 1897, he enrolled at Princeton University in 1915 and two years later put his name down for the fledging Aviation Corps. "They are organizing here," Vaughn wrote his parents on February 7, 1917. "But [I] don't know whether I will be able to get in it or not, as they are going to have examinations for nerves, endurance, etc."

Vaughn had to wait a couple of months for his medical examination, by which time the Princeton Aviation School had been firmly established and war had been formally declared by Congress. "Committees composed of members of the Faculty and of the undergraduates were formed," reported the *Princeton Bric-a-Brac*, the university's undergraduate yearbook. "Several members of the Faculty volunteered to give lectures on the construction, operation and maintenance of an airplane motor . . . [and] towards the end of March came the gratifying announcement that sufficient funds had been collected and orders for two airplanes of the Curtiss JN-4B type of military tractor biplane were at once placed with the Curtiss Aeroplane Company."

Vaughn underwent his physical examination in April, the doctor noting the cadet's brown hair, blue eyes, and ruddy complexion in his file. Vaughn wrote his family on May 4 to explain that after undergoing the equilibrium and eye test, he had been subjected to a thorough

George Vaughn was an ace with thirteen victories who lived to be ninety-two. "All you had to do was fly the plane and shoot the guns," he said modestly, shortly before his death.

medical "that has put a good many fellows out of the Corps. It was a physical examination such as I never even imagined before, and lasted over two hours and a half. You have to be practically perfect in every part of your body to get by, so I at least have the satisfaction of knowing that I am physically pretty well off."

Vaughn was one of thirty-six Princeton men out of more than one hundred volunteers who passed the medical, as was Elliott White Springs. "They are very particular about whom they take for the Aviation Corps and examine us very minutely," Springs had written his father on May 1. "It's the most exacting examination the Army gives. They spin you around on a stool, make you balance blindfolded, fire pistols behind you and all sorts of things like that."

Springs confessed to his father that he'd feared his eyes might let him down—"as they only allow a small percentage of variations from normal"—but he passed the medical, unlike Arthur Taber, who failed his. Though an enthusiastic rower and member of the Princeton gun team, the portly young man lacked finesse and aggression. He didn't lack connections, however, not with so wealthy and influential a father. The dean of the college, Howard McClenahan, wrote to the Aviation Corps to tell them of the student's "strictest integrity," while Taber also paid a visit to Washington "and called on a friend . . . a retired Brigadier-General, whose help in attaining this object he asked."

At first the RFC resisted the pressure to accept Taber, but, finally, they relented and he was admitted into the Princeton Aviation School in July, by which time Vaughn and Springs and their thirty-four classmates were already accomplished aviators. "I can't begin to tell you the wonderful fascination of flying and I enjoy it more every time I go up," Springs wrote his father. "I had control of the plane yesterday for twenty minutes at an altitude of 4,000 feet and I don't know when I enjoyed anything more."

The students were taught in the Curtiss JN-4 biplanes on what Vaughn described as "a privately-operated field, located between

Elliot White Springs beams for the camera after walking away unscathed from this flying accident in France.

Princeton and Lawrenceville," and it was here that Taber joined them, if not trusted to take to the skies, then at least able to participate in "such subjects as theory of flight, internal combustion engines, machine guns, Morse code telegraphy, navigation, etc." The students, most of whom had hitherto led lives of easy deportment, also encountered military discipline and close order drill for the first time. "All this drill was excessively tiresome and a dreadful bore," Taber wrote his father on July 26. ". . . I sometimes regret that I did not join the naval aviation for in that branch now I could make a greater contribution to the Allied cause than where I am."

With the six-week course complete and the cadets now "enlisted as Privates First Class in the Aviation Section of the Signal Corps," the army faced the problem of what to do with them. "At that time there were no advanced flying schools in this country," recalled Vaughn. "Fortunately for us, the Allies had started offering the use of their flying training facilities, so the army finally decided to send us abroad for advanced flying training."

At the end of August the Princeton cadets were sent to Mineola flying field on Long Island, later the site of the Roosevelt Raceway, where they encountered cadets from other flying schools also waiting to embark overseas, some to France and others to Italy.

For Arthur Taber the stay at the Mineola airfield was his first exposure to the rich diversity of his country's inhabitants. Reared in Lake Forest, Illinois, and schooled in Coconut Grove, Florida, the formative years of Taber's young life had been spent in a privileged and serene environment. Earnest and studious, Taber entered Princeton, where he was a member of the university's gun team, which contested an intercollegiate shoot with teams representing Dartmouth, Yale, and Cornell. This was the circle in which Taber felt comfortable: among the wealthy and well-educated, among America's elite.

On August 28, his first evening at Mineola, Taber wrote his father, explaining: "This seems to be a concentration point for the men who are going to Italy: today a batch came in from Cornell. They are a clean-cut, military-looking lot, and I am rather heartened by their appearance. They are surely exceptional in being trim in appearance, for the average is very low, I regret to say."

Taber had no issue with the Cornell men, nor with fellow Princetonians such as George Vaughn, Frank Dixon, Harold Bulkley, and Elliott Springs, even if Springs did have something of a wild reputation. At Princeton, he had spent much of his time striking a pose in his Stutz Bearcat, even driving the vehicle to Long Island when they were ordered to Mineola.

However, at least Springs—the son of a wealthy cotton-mill owner from South Carolina—had breeding. Taber wasn't so sure of some of Springs's acquaintances, budding aviators who had been ordered to Mineola from other flying schools across America. Clayton Knight, a native of Rochester, New York, and, at twenty-six, one of the oldest men at Mineola, was an artist who had studied under the iconoclastic modernist painter Robert Henri before enlisting in the military in 1917 and being sent to aviation school in Texas.

But if Knight was tainted by association in the eyes of Taber, John McGavock Grider was tainted, period. Born in 1892 at the family cotton plantation in Sans Souci, Arkansas, Grider—or "Mac" as he preferred to be called—had quit the Memphis University School aged seventeen to marry a fellow student, Miss Marguerite Samuels. To escape the scandal, Grider and his young bride retreated to the plantation, where she soon gave birth to two sons, John McGavock and George William. Neither Grider nor his wife adapted well to parenthood; he was working all hours on the plantation, and she found the responsibility too much to bear. The couple separated, Marguerite returning to her family in Memphis with the children, Grider throwing himself into his work. But he was still young and restless, and America's entry into the Great War was the excuse he needed to flee Arkansas. Writing his family of his decision to enlist, he said: "Do you think I'm going to tell John and George when they get to be men that I raised cotton and corn during the war? Not by a damned sight, I'm going to tell them I raised hell."

Grider was sent to the School of Military Aeronautics of the University of Illinois for aviation training, during which he wrote a friend back home of his first flight. "I have been up. God it is wonderful! I have never experienced anything like it in my life."

One of the "Three Musketeers," Laurence Callahan was not just a brilliant ragtime pianist but also an ace with 85 Squadron and 148th Aero.

Grider's roommate was Larry Callahan, a tall, laid-back twenty-three-year-old from Kentucky who had curtailed a career in finance to serve his country. The pair hit it off straight away. Callahan was a gifted pianist and Grider loved to dance, the foxtrot being his favorite. They also shared a passion for liquor, women, and cards. Such pastimes were not the preserve of Taber. "I am not a prude about the question of drinking," he wrote his father, "but I don't like to see men take too much, first, because of the dire result of their actions upon themselves, and secondly, because someone else is sure to suffer, for some regrettable thing never fails to occur when one is temporarily and abnormally excited."

Grider and Callahan were separated upon arrival at Mineola. Grider, like Taber, had volunteered for active service in Italy, while Callahan had been assigned to the contingent headed to France. The Italian detachment had as its cadet sergeant Elliott Springs, confident and strong willed despite having just turned twenty-one. A natural leader and a superb aviator, Springs was invested with the limited authority by the officer in charge, Maj. Leslie MacDill, with instructions to ensure the men did nothing to discredit America in the eyes of the watching world.

It was an onerous task for Springs, an exuberant and forceful personality whose character had been shaped in a large part by his prickly relationship with his domineering father. "I am opposed to your joining the aviation corps," Leroy Springs had written his son in April 1917. "I do not feel that I should give my consent to it." Aviation was the younger Springs's escape from parental control, a joy he described in a letter to his stepmother as "the nearest thing to the Balm of Gilead I know."

But there were other balms in Springs's life: the same pleasures enjoyed by Grider. At Mineola, Grider discovered that Springs played bridge and liked music, so he told him, "I have a friend over here at this other place that's a good bridge player and plays the piano. You better get him over here." The friend in question was Callahan. Springs did as requested, arranging the transfer of Callahan to the Italian detachment of aviators. The three young men complemented each other: the blond, handsome Grider, the eldest of the three but with an infectious boyish enthusiasm for life; Springs, who looked like a boy, his face unmarked by toil or trauma, but whose personality was more complex than either Grider's or Callahan's; and Callahan, who asked himself fewer questions than his two friends and just got on with life, taking its vagaries in his languid stride. Before long the trio were calling themselves "the Three Musketeers."

A reporter from the *New York Times* ventured to Mineola to spend several days in the company of the cadets and captured the tedium felt by many of the raw recruits in an article entitled "Long, Weary Waiting for Airplane Student." "The first sight of the high board inclosure [*sic*] of the flying field brings a distinct thrill," wrote the correspondent. "But after sitting in barracks day after day, fingering brand-new equipment, cleaning brand-new pistols, hearing the airplanes of the fortunate buzz by overhead, ever and again sneezing in the plentiful dust—that yellow Long Island dust which rises so thickly when the ground is scratched that even the general's car must slow down on the high road—well, that thrill wears off."[6]

[6] The article was eventually published on October 7, 1917, and when it finally reached Springs in England he commented in a letter home, "'Twas rather good."

As for the cadets who sat listlessly in the classroom, desperate to fly but damned to spend hour after hour studying theory, the reporter from the *New York Times* sympathized with their plight, writing: "The men who have volunteered for training in Italy are in a curious state of mind. They have no idea of where they are going or of what is going to happen to them when they get there; but they are perfectly sure that it will be the best possible. No one has been sent to Italy for flying training yet, or at least no one has been there long enough to send back word what it is like, and these men will be the first in that particular field, pioneers, explorers. And that is enough."

On Sunday, September 16, 1917, Major MacDill ordered Springs to tell "everyone to get rid of their cars" except for Springs himself and to "place sentinels around the barracks to keep anyone from leaving even for a few moments." MacDill and Springs then drove into New York to "arrange the final details" of their embarkation for Europe, and the following day, September 17, Springs deposited his treasured Stutz at the Blue Sprocket garage with instructions for it to be returned to the manufacturer. Springs then drew some money, dined out at a fashionable restaurant, and returned to Mineola at 2:00 a.m. "to find special orders waiting on me to have breakfast at 4:30 and be ready to break up camp at 6:30."

A Curtiss-Herring at Mineola airfield in the early days of aviation. *Library of Congress*

Springs did as instructed, and at 7:00 a.m. on Tuesday, September 18, he and approximately 150 other cadets boarded a train bound for Long Island City. Once they arrived, remembered George Vaughn, they were taken on a tugboat to SS *Carmania* of the Cunard Line. "Since there were not supposed to be any troops abroad, we were boarded via rope ladders on the river side, where we could not be seen from the dock."

Carmania wasn't the first vessel to transport American aviators across the Atlantic to Europe. A month earlier RMS *Aurania* had sailed from New York to Liverpool with a detachment of fifty two cadets under the command of Capt. Geoffrey Dwyer, including 1st Lts. Bennett Oliver and Paul Winslow, both of whom had been obliged to take their turn on watch, their eyes scanning the gray ocean for signs of dreaded German submarines. Half an hour before midnight on August 30, Winslow had spotted a light in the distance. "It was Ireland," he wrote in his diary, "and nothing ever seemed so good as the sight of something indicating land, as it meant we were safe once more."

The mood among the second contingent of American flyers destined for Europe was carefree; the men were unconcerned by the prospect of submarine attack. After nearly three weeks of being stranded at Mineola they were finally on their way to war, and wrapped tight around them as they scaled *Carmania*'s rope ladders was the invincibility of youth.

Carmania, launched in 1905, was the pride of the Cunard fleet, powered by steam turbines with a speed of eighteen knots. The aviators were shown to their quarters in first class along with a handful of civilian passengers, some army officers, and forty Red Cross nurses. "The boat we have is a very good one," wrote Vaughn to his family. "There are a lot of regulars with us, mostly infantry, and all riding in the steerage, and I guess it is not too pleasant down there."

For Vaughn and his fellow aviators, however, the voyage was "just like a vacation trip for us; lots of sleep, excellent food, deck chairs and all our time to ourselves."

Once she left New York on Tuesday, September 18, *Carmania* headed north to Halifax, Nova Scotia, where it arrived two days later, joining a convoy of ships teeming with New Zealand infantrymen.

The following day, September 21, the fourteen-strong convoy slipped out of Halifax and into the Atlantic. "As we came thru from the inner basin down the river south to the sea we passed the British battle cruisers, their bands all playing 'the Star Spangled Banner,'" wrote Grider in his diary, "and their crews cheering with their well-organized 'Hip Hurrah,' the 'Hip' being given by an officer thru a megaphone. As we were coming out of the inner basin, one of our convoy steamed past us with one lone bugler playing our national anthem and everyone on board standing rigidly at attention. I never had quite such a thrill from the old tune before."

With North America behind them, the aviators settled into a routine for the twelve-day passage to England. The only disagreeable part of the day was the hour of calisthenics each morning, led by Springs, who also oversaw a daily boat drill each afternoon. Otherwise the aviators could do as they please. "The only distinction between us and the regular first class passengers is our uniform," wrote Vaughn.

There were daily Italian lessons, taught either by Capt. Fiorello LaGuardia, a New York congressman who had enlisted in the Aviation Section, Signal Corps, following the outbreak of war; or Albert Spalding, a celebrated concert pianist with the New York Symphony and an enlisted man when he first boarded the *Carmania*. But upon hearing of Spalding's presence, Springs persuaded Major MacDill "to move him up from steerage to a vacant stateroom." La Guardia brought with him two of his ward bosses as cooks, and soon Springs was writing his parents to explain that, despite the daily calisthenics, he was "getting fat as a pig."

If the men weren't eating or exercising or learning Italian, they were enjoying the ship's myriad activities. "We have the usual shipboard games, shuffle board, etc., to amuse us," wrote Vaughn. "All kinds of deck chairs, reading rooms, smoking rooms and lounges to sit around in."

What better place than a deck chair or smoking room for the 150 aviators to become better acquainted, to swap stories, and to compare experiences of their introduction to flight?

As *Carmania* made steady progress toward Europe, the young aviators who weren't on submarine watch or confined to their cabins by seasickness continued to exchange experiences. They compared notes on what they'd been taught at ground school about active service: how a pilot "must be constantly on the alert against attack from below, behind and above as well as from in front"; the importance of watching the wind in case its direction should turn; the necessity of always having "a landing field in sight in case the motor goes bad"; how an aircraft's machine gun is not accurate beyond three hundred yards;

and, most important of all, the fact that an airplane "is usually invisible when it is on your level and over two miles away." What that meant, the instructors had drummed into their pupils, is that should you glance over your shoulder for seven seconds to check for hostile aircraft, an enemy in front of you "would have *passed* you although it was out of sight when you first turned round! Such a thing is easily possible with a speed of 120 mph."[7]

As *Carmania* approached the west coast of Ireland, some of the men sat down to write letters home, ready to mail them the moment they stepped ashore. On October 1, George Vaughn wrote his family, "I think we will probably land to-morrow, and I will start writing now, in order to send this off as soon as possible." He went on to describe the voyage, the games they played, the Italian they learned, and the "excellent" food they enjoyed. As to the future, Vaughn explained that none of them knew what that held: "Even the major [MacDill] does not know what we do or where we go when we land so I cannot say much anyway . . . [Y]ou will know everything is o.k. when you get it through, and that is all that is necessary. Will write again as soon as possible."

Elliott Springs was in an ebullient mood when he wrote his stepmother on the eve of their arrival in Europe. "Gee, it's great to be alive and you can't imagine how rosy this existence has become. I feel like a prince now," he began, concluding, "I feel now that I can make good and all I want is a chance to do it. I have gotten away with this so far and it's given me unbounded confidence in myself that it will take a lot to shake."

The emotions of John McGavock Grider were less bullish, more melancholic. A few months earlier, down in hot, sultry Arkansas, he had written his sisters of his wish to go to Europe to "raise hell." It was easy to be brave thousands of miles from the frontline. But now he was about to arrive in Europe, where, for over three years, men had been slaughtering each other in unimaginable numbers. Nearly two weeks at sea had given Grider ample time to think—about his life thus far, about the future, and about the two young boys he had left far behind. "There's a full moon tonight and the sea is beautiful," he wrote in his diary. "Oh for words to describe it! it makes me sad and makes me ache inside for something, I don't know what. I guess

[7] Sydney Taber, *Arthur Richmond Taber*

it's a little loving I need. . . . I have always longed for better things but didn't know how to go about getting them. But now Fate has tossed me this opportunity. I must make the best of it! All I have to pay for it is my life."

On October 1, as they came within sight of Ireland, Grider wrote his youngest son, George, on the day of his fifth birthday:

> Dear little George or should I say big George, now it's your birthday. Don't you feel big? I wish daddy could see you and give you five big kisses and a hug. I want you to know daddy is thinking of his boys tonight and of you sweet child. I remembered your birthday and am enclosing some money for mamma to buy a present with. Daddy is on a big ship now, going across the ocean and when you get this you will know he's gotten across safely and is in Italy, flying an aeroplane and thinking of his darling little boys at home. If I had you and John here I would be perfectly happy. I may come home next fall, son, and you and John must be good and learn how to read and write lots of things. I bet you have grown a foot. I would rather see you both tonight than anyone in the world.
>
> George, you and John must never forget me. And never forget that I love you better than anyone else in the world.

CHAPTER 2

The Suicide Club

SS *Carmania* docked at Liverpool, on the northwest coast of England, at 8:00 on the morning of October 2, 1917. There was a surprise in store for the aviators when they disembarked, and it wasn't only the weather, which Clayton Knight described as "pretty raw" after a summer spent in the Texas heat. As the 150 aviators stood on the quay, "our packs on our backs and suitcases in hand," cold but excited, Major MacDill called Elliott Springs to one side to break the news that he himself had just received. "Springs," he told his cadet sergeant. "We're not going to Italy. You're to stay here and train in England, and Captain LaGuardia and myself and the doctors and enlisted men are ordered to report to Paris. I'm sorry."

Sorry as he was, MacDill delegated the task of telling the men to his subordinate and then told Springs to take the men 150 miles south to Oxford, in central England, where they would be billeted with the first contingent of American aviators who had arrived the previous month.

Springs took a deep breath, gathered his fellow aviators around him, and announced the news that, instead of admiring exotic women under the Italian sun, they would be spending their days at Oxford, pretty in its own way but not at all what the men had been anticipating.

"The men simply went wild when I told them," Springs wrote his father a few days later. "The swearing must have been heard in Berlin!" Arthur Taber told his father "there was a near riot" when Springs broke the news, adding, "It was a stunning blow, and a most disastrous one for the morale of the corps."

Not all the aviators were so distraught. John McGavock Grider admitted to his diary his irritation at having wasted several hours learning Italian, but other than that and the fact they would be obliged to change their Italian lira into pounds sterling, he had little problem with the change in plan. The train journey south from Liverpool to Oxford took Grider "through the most beautiful country I ever saw," and both he and George Vaughn were amazed by the reception accorded them as they sped through the English countryside. "The people all along the line came out of their houses and waved to us as we passed," Vaughn wrote his family. "I have never seen so much enthusiasm as is shown here."

Waiting to greet the Americans in Oxford was the first contingent of aviators, who had commenced their RFC ground school on September 4. Paul Winslow, a twenty-five-year-old from Cook County, Illinois, had taken a while to become accustomed to his new way of life and the British way of doing things. Classes ended each day at 7.30 p.m., by which time it was dark, making it a challenge to return to one's billets in a country blacked out as a precaution against enemy air raids. "We are lined up, the air ringing with the crisp, sharp commands of the English," he wrote in his diary. The colonel led the cadets off, marching in front of two detachments of British cadets, with the Americans bringing up the rear. "We go third, and it is ludicrous to try and keep in step with the 140 [step-per-minute] cadence of the English, when ours is 120. We look like a huge accordion going down the street."

As Elliott Springs led his cadets through the ancient streets of Oxford, it wasn't the marching speed that almost caused their first casualties of the war. "I nearly got the whole bunch run over by not keeping on the left hand side of the streets," remarked Springs in a letter home. Springs and his men were billeted in Christ Church College, originally founded in 1524 by Cardinal Wolsey, one of King Henry VIII's most trusted advisors, and just a quarter of a mile from where Winslow and the other Americans were housed in another part of the university, Queens College.

Such was the hospitality lavished upon them in Oxford that the Americans soon forgot all about Italy. John McGavock Grider shared a room with Larry Callahan, Jim Stokes, and Elliott Springs, and he delighted not just in their surroundings—"Our mess hall is like a chapel with stained glass windows and the most wonderful paintings all around"—but also the fact that champagne was served with their meals.

Springs, still restrained by the responsibility of leadership, marveled at the way the Americans had been treated "like princes" and added: "These English people are wonderful . . . and they are all sportsmen, through and through. I've had tea at several estates nearby and the women all seem to have the same attitude. And they'll certainly never quit until there's nobody to fight with. I wish I'd gotten into it sooner."

Springs admitted his surprise at the youth of the British cadets training alongside the Americans at Oxford, as did George Vaughn in a letter home dated October 10, 1917. Most, he said, were only eighteen or nineteen, before going on to describe life in England: "Our first class is at 8:30 in the morning, and we work from that time until 12:45, when we come home for lunch. After lunch we can do what we please until 4:15, when we go back to classes, and study until 6:45. Then we have dinner, and have a study period from 8:30 until 11 o'clock, which gives us a chance to write letters, etc."

In one such letter, written on October 24, Arthur Taber told his parents he was now midway through the six-week ground course, and benefiting immensely from the tutelage. "The instruction is splendid both in method and clarity," he wrote. "Everything which can possibly help a student to understand mechanism or construction or whatever the subject may be is taken advantage of; he is given the actual object to inspect or, if this is not practicable, a model in miniature is provided. He is further aided by diagrams, cross-sectional drawings, photographs, lantern-slides, pictures, printed notes, etc., etc. Most of the work is done in small classes consisting of seven, eight or nine men in each class. This gives everyone ample opportunity to ask questions, inspect models, etc."

There were also lectures on enemy aircraft identification, aerial bombs, artillery observation, wireless, physics and chemistry, and on "all kinds of engines—of both rotary and stationary types." There were practical classes in gunnery for which the students were escorted to the firing range and let loose on the Vickers machine gun, since 1916 the standard weapon on British aircraft because its closed-bolt firing cycle made it easier to synchronize with the propeller than the Lewis gun.

The more the American cadets became immersed in the training so the more they considered themselves part of the RFC and not the Aviation Section of the U.S. Signal Corps. They bought English boots and leather belts from the officers' store in Oxford, and some—notably Springs—took to wearing British tunics with lapel collars instead of the

The Lewis gun, seen here, was gradually replaced on British aircraft by the Vickers gun, whose closed-bolt firing cycle made it easier to synchronize with the propeller.

U.S. Army–issue stand-up collars. They were also issued with RFC caps bordered with the white cadet band, and they adhered to the behavior expected of a British officer. "We are not allowed, for instance, to have anything to do with soldiers or enlisted men in public," wrote Vaughn. "We must be very neat in our appearance, must not walk on the streets in groups of more than three fellows, must never be seen standing

American cadets arriving in England often adopted local customs, wearing the RFC cap and exchanging their U.S. army–issue stand-up collars for the British tunics with lapel collars, as seen on this British flying officer.

around in the streets but must always have some definite object in view, or appear to have."

Despite the hospitality, the thorough instruction, and the novelty of acting like British officers, an air of restlessness still clung to the cloisters of Christ Church College. Nearly a month after arriving in England not one of the aviators had actually flown. To burn off the excess energy a boxing tournament was staged—the 200-pound Grider fought a brutal bout with a cadet named Joe Sharpe—and on Saturday, October 27, a party was thrown to celebrate one of the men's birthdays. "It was a regular riot," wrote Springs, and it was all the more

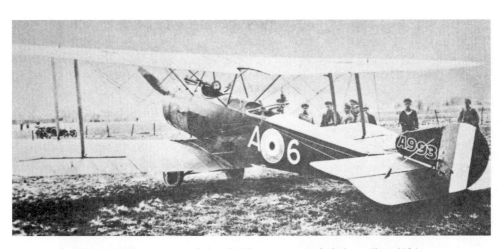

Despite its rotary 130-horsepower engine, the Sopwith 1½ Strutter was easy prey for the German Albatros D.I fighters.

so because they joined forces with the first contingent of American aviators, who were celebrating the end of their course at Oxford. Paul Winslow was among those present, along with his brother, Alan, on leave in England from service in France with the Lafayette Flying Corps, those American aviators serving with the French.

Before the party Winslow had told some of the cadets, including Grider, that over in France "the Hun [German] has the supremacy of the air." This hadn't always been the case. The fall and winter of 1915–1916 had belonged to the Germans, thanks to their introduction of the Fokker *Eindecker*, a monoplane with a Parabellum machine gun mounted on its cowling. It was better than anything the RFC possessed and led British pilots to curse the "Fokker Scourge" for their inferiority. Yet the Germans failed to drive home their technical advantage, spreading the *Eindecker* among squadrons rather than building one devastating, large-scale fighter unit.

By spring 1916 the air war was beginning to swing back the way of the Allies, as the French Nieuport 11 fighters, together with the British de Havilland 2 (Airco DH.2) and the Farman Experimental 2 (Royal Aircraft Factory F.E.2) two-seater biplane, stood up to the *Eindeckers*. Then came the Sopwith 1½ Strutter, followed in September 1916 by the Sopwith Pup, the most effective British fighter to date.

However, the Allies' superiority was short lived. In fall 1916, the Albatros D.II made its first appearance over the Western Front; this aircraft was a modification on the D.I, a machine about whose poor visibility the pilots had complained. To remedy this defect, the

Baron Manfred von Richthofen, the ace of aces of the First World War.

D.IIs were manufactured with the upper wing closer to the fuselage, on which were mounted two synchronous Spandau machine guns.

But it wasn't just the machines that handed the advantage back to the Germans in early 1917. Their air force had been reorganized in the summer of 1916, resulting in the introduction of a fourteen-strong fighter squadron, known to the Germans as the *Jagdstaffel* (*Jasta*). Oswald Boelcke was the commander of *Jasta* 2 when it became operational in September, and although he was killed in October 1916, by April 1917 a total of thirty-seven *Jastas* had been formed.

Of all the *Jasta* pilots none was successful as Manfred von Richthofen, a protégé of Boelcke, who said of his mentor, "Whatever Boelcke told us was taken as Gospel."

Boelcke produced a set of rules for his pilots, known as his *Dicta*, one of which was: "Foolish acts of bravery only bring death. The *Jasta* must fight as a unit with close teamwork between all pilots. The signal of its leaders must be obeyed."

The twenty-four-year-old Richthofen, who volunteered for the air force having first served in a cavalry regiment, learned quickly from Boelcke. By the time *Jasta* 2 lost its commander in a flying accident, Richthofen had already shot down six British aircraft in the space of five weeks. Richthofen enjoyed the adulation that grew with every enemy machine downed in his Albatros D.III, the latest German fighter aircraft first seen in France in December 1916. He painted the fuselage of his Albatros bright red and reveled in the name bestowed on him by the British as a result—the Red Baron. French pilots preferred to call him *le diable rouge* (the Red Devil), but they had less cause to fear the German than the RFC: Richthofen's favored prey flew British machines, and seven months after his first kill, he had shot down more than fifty RFC aircraft. "One of the Englishmen

Manfred von Richthofen held the Albatros D.III in high regard from the outset and painted his machine bright red, leading his enemies to dub him "the Red Baron."

whom we had shot down and whom we had made a prisoner was talking with us," Richthofen would later write in his autobiography, *Der Rote Kampfflieger*. "Of course he inquired after the Red Airplane. It is not unknown even among the troops in the trenches and is called by them the 'diable rouge.' In the squadron to which he belonged there was a rumor that the Red Machine was occupied by a girl, by a kind of Jeanne d'Arc. He was intensely surprised when I assured him that the supposed girl was standing in front of him. He did not intend to make a joke. He was actually convinced that only a girl could sit in the extravagantly painted machine."

Winslow's sobering disclosure about Germany's dominance of the skies over France served to make the cadets savor the party more than ever. "Everybody was all teed up before they got there and we had cocktails by the quart and champagne and then each man got a half gallon pitcher of ale," Grider wrote in his diary.

The alcohol flowed, and so did the mischief, among the British cadets as much as their American brothers-in-arms. The colonel of the ground school, arriving to break up the party, was pushed to the ground by a British officer, and mayhem ensued. As the colonel roared in indignation, the cadets scattered to the four winds. He caught one, Paul Winslow, and marched him back to his billet with the intention of discovering his original assailant. "They say it was the greatest sight that Oxford ever witnessed," Grider gleefully wrote. "Sixty American

Harold Bulkley was Vaughn's great buddy who was killed in a training accident in February 1918 while serving with 85 Squadron.

soldiers in all sorts of costumes, in all stages of drunkenness, trying to get into line and stay there, in a dark and ancient courtyard, hallowed by the scholars of the ages, with a British colonel dashing about with a flashlight and bellowing like a bull at each man."

The colonel failed to discover his assailant but it was surely no coincidence that a week later, Saturday November 3, the 150 American aviators left Oxford. It fell to Elliott Springs to select twenty cadets among their number for flight instruction at Stamford (approximately eighty-five miles north of Oxford) while the rest were to report to gunnery ground school at Grantham, a market town one hundred miles north of Oxford.

Springs found the task of selecting the twenty cadets "agony." Every cadet wanted to begin flight instruction and not spend more weeks on another course, and for his part there was nothing Springs wanted more than to take his fellow "musketeers"—Larry Callahan and John McGavock Grider—to Stamford, particularly as once there he would be just another cadet and not their sergeant as he had been at Oxford. But Springs's conscientiousness won out and, as he told his father, "I finally closed my eyes to friendship and prejudice" and selected seventeen members of the Princeton Aviation Corps with the other three cadets—Roy Garver, Philip Dietz, and William Deetjen chosen for the "considerable clerical work" at Oxford.[8]

At least that way he could claim to have made his choice on cold, hard facts—that he had seen the majority of the Princeton cadets fly and knew their capabilities. George Vaughn was among the chosen, as was Arthur Taber, a curiosity considering he had not actually flown at Princeton. Springs may have been protecting Taber, or he may have already concluded that his classmate was not fighter pilot material and would be wasting his time on a gunnery course. Better

[8] All three cadets were subsequently killed flying.

to train him up as a pilot so he could eventually find some role for which he was suited.

Vaughn was delighted to be chosen, as was his best friend, twenty-year-old Harold Bulkley, a New Jersey native who had captained Princeton's freshman tennis team. On Friday November 9, Vaughn wrote his family to tell them of his new address in Stamford and declare: "We are being treated royally here, even better than we were at Oxford. . . . [T]he meals are wonderful, almost equal to the *Carmania*, and we are living in a vacant private house."

The following week Vaughn wrote again, this letter breathless with excitement: "At last we have started flying, and owing to our previous training some of us are flying alone now. I was up for about an hour and a half to-day."

A few days later Vaughn boasted in a letter that "I have had about ten hours 'solo' [flying] now, in about five days, which is pretty good for November weather."

Springs was also banking many hours of flying time, his confidence bolstered by the fact the RFC were using the same Curtiss JN-4 aircraft that he'd flown at Princeton. On November 12, Springs flew solo for fifteen minutes, reaching a height of seven hundred meters. The next day he soloed for one hour and fifteen minutes, and went up as high as four thousand meters, and on November 14, he flew alone for one hour and forty minutes. Like Vaughn, Springs wrote only briefly in a letter to his family of his first solo flight. Despite his jubilation at the feat, Vaughn knew people back home wouldn't understand; no one would understand except that small band of intrepid men who had themselves flown solo. It was a monumental moment in every aviator's life, as Paul Winslow—also training at Stamford—confided to his diary on November 15:

I taxied out alone. It was a queer feeling but I had no fear, only a little shaky. After heading into the wind I waited until the end of the field was entirely clear of machines, gave her the gun and off we went—not a bump . . . when we reached a safe height, I managed to remember to throttle back to 1300 RPM's and began to feel at home, look around and watch the instruments, etc. When we reached 600ft I made a very conservative turn, straightened out and felt fine. Now I know why birds sing. I actually did and didn't realize it. Having circled the field . . . down went the nose, off went the engine and we sailed at the earth. Suddenly, the ground came up close and unconsciously I pulled back on the stick and we landed without a quiver, by chance, and I taxied in feeling like a trained aviator with long experience. When I neared the hangar, the lieutenant came and congratulated me. My first solo was completed, thank God. It was wonderful sport, though, and I itch for another ride.

Arthur Taber wasn't quite so as proficient. On December 6 he wrote his parents from Stamford, explaining that he soon hoped to go solo but for the moment "I have had over five hours' instruction on dual control." He admitted this was "shockingly little . . . but is accounted for by the facts that we had many classes to go to at first, that the weather has been treacherous, and that there had been a scarcity of machines, as well as a lack of enthusiasm for flying on the part of instructors."

Taber was clearly lying. Springs had flown more than twenty-three hours one week in late November, which he said was pretty good "considering that the weather's been bad—foggy every day." He'd got lost on one occasion, as had most of the cadets, but wasn't that all part of the learning experience?

By mid-December, Vaughn and Bulkley had mastered the arts of looping and spinning, which, as Vaughn explained to his family, "consists of getting the machine in such a position that it is diving vertically, and revolving about its longitudinal axis at the same time." As their flight instructors told them, spinning was an effective way to shake off an enemy aircraft in combat.

Combat was what most of the cadets relished and for Springs the prospect drew nearer when he was posted to 74 Squadron of the RFC on November 24.

Springs was the first of the *Carmania* contingent to graduate from flying school, and he arrived at his new squadron at London Colney—twenty miles north of central London—on November 25. Reporting to his flight commander, Springs quickly realized he was no longer the star attraction, the leading cadet, but just another novice in a fighter squadron preparing for combat in France. Springs was asked for details of next of kin and how best to contact them, and one of the sergeants "asked if I had been disappointed in love or was I a consumptive. I fled to the bar in horror."

The sergeant had meant no offence. He had simply been curious to know why Springs, an American, had joined the RFC—the "Suicide Club" as it was better known. The RFC was still recovering from the

"Bloody April" of a few months earlier, when in the space of thirty days Britain's air service had lost 151 aircraft and 316 crew. New pilots, such as Springs, had a life expectancy of seventeen days; in some squadrons it was as little as eleven.

Who in their right minds, wondered the sergeant, would actually be *eager* to see combat? Not the British, war-weary after three bloody years of war; nor the French, whose army had mutinied earlier in 1917 in protest at their callous and incompetent leaders; and not the Russians, whose Bolshevik leader, Vladimir Lenin, was just about to sign an armistice with Germany.

The only enthusiastic power in the war was the United States, whose soldiers, sailors, and airmen had read of the great war but not yet experienced it first hand. Springs was in the vanguard of the American military, bright-eyed and belligerent and, as he told his parents, "itching to get at the Boche," his naivety a source of amusement—but also a comfort—to his British allies.

For Springs wasn't the first American to fight with the RFC. Though some of his compatriots had gained a formidable reputation flying with France's Lafayette squadron, a small number of American aviators had been distinguishing themselves in British squadrons while Springs had still been cruising around Princeton in his red Stutz Bearcat.

CHAPTER 3

The King and the Cowboy

On Friday November 2, 1917, the same month that Elliott Springs was posted to 74 Squadron, the *Repository* newspaper in Canton, Ohio, carried a photo of Captain Frederick Libby, under which was an article describing him as an "American ace of British fliers." Libby was in the news because he was in the United States, no longer a member of the RFC but a newly appointed instructor in the Aviation Section, Signal Corps.

Libby had actually arrived in New York a fortnight before the article appeared. With him was another American aviator who had flown in the RFC, Captain Norman Read. The pair split for the weekend, with Libby accepting the hospitality of his cousin at his Long Island home. When Read and Libby met up on the Monday morning, they took a train to Washington to report to the Signal Corps. On the train south they described their weekends. Neither had much good to say about the experiences. "They all want to hear horrible things," said Libby. "Certainly, the war is no picnic, but who the hell wants to talk about war all of the time, just to satisfy curious people?" In short, he added, "small-town talk gives me a pain in my rear." Read agreed. It would be good to be back among military men.

The next day Libby and Read reported to the adjutant general's office in Washington. They received a glacial welcome from a major who didn't deign to get to his feet. Nor did he ask about their experience in France, or show any interest in their backgrounds. Instead he

The intrepid Fred Libby claimed fourteen kills with the British, most as an observer and most before America had even entered the war.

told the pair they must shed their British uniforms, swear an oath of allegiance to America, and then start at the bottom as junior military aviators without wings, training on Curtiss Jennys. It was all too much for Read. "In a language this bird can understand [he] tells him to shove his wings, the Jenny and his damn commission where it will do the most good," recalled Libby. Then Read jumped to his feet, banged the desk of the startled major and yelled: "Your treatment of us today is unbelievable! Libby has had two years of RFC in four fighting squadrons, has more hours in the air and more enemy ships to his credit than any American. All of this you must know. He is the only American with a real record."

Born in the small cowtown of Sterling, Colorado, in the summer of 1892, Libby experienced his first tragedy before he turned four. His mother died, and young Fred was reared by his father and his big brother, Bud, who taught him how to break horses to ride. By the time he was eighteen, Fred Libby was breaking horses for a living in the Mazatzal Mountains in Arizona. In the years that followed, the horses, and his sense of adventure, took Libby to Colorado, New Mexico, and Washington State. In the summer of 1914 Libby and a friend took a train to Calgary where they heard the Canadian government would offer good support to people wanting to work on the land. Libby had it in mind to build a ranch, but, a few weeks after his arrival in Calgary, Canada and the rest of the British Empire declared war on Germany.

The war had nothing to do with Libby but he sauntered over anyway to one of the many recruiting rallies in Calgary, curious about the crowd of young men gathered outside. "Three dollars and thirty cents a day, every day including Saturday and Sunday, with everything furnished, a chance to travel, starting immediately, tomorrow, no training required."[9] Hell, thought Libby, when he learned of the deal, why not? He had just turned twenty-two, had no ties or responsibilities, and no reason to idle away his youth in North America while over in Europe was the chance to taste glory in war.

Less than a year later Libby was in France with a Canadian motorized unit, trying to reconcile himself to the fact that it was his own choice that he was up to his knees in mud.[10] "Such rain I have never seen," he wrote in his memoirs. "With water everywhere, it is impossible to keep dry, and along with the weather there are the damned rats, cooties and, just a rock's throw away, our enemy, the Hun."

Then, in early 1916, Libby spotted a notice pinned to the bulletin board of his unit's orderly room. The notice sought volunteers for the RFC, specifically observers who would be given a thirty days' trial with the possibility of a commission at the end of that period. Libby knew nothing about airplanes, nor what an observer was required to do, other than "observe" something, but he did know one thing: "It might be a nice way out of this damn rain."

Libby put his name forward, and, a few days later, he was standing before a colonel in the RFC. The British officer asked Libby what he knew about airplanes. "Absolutely nothing," replied the American, but

---

[9] Frederick Libby, *Horses Don't Fly*

[10] There is some confusion as to the exact date Libby actually volunteered as his enlistment papers are dated January 1915.

explained that he could break a horse. The colonel roared with delight, "as he was the owner of several polo ponies." The interview took on a more equine nature and, at its conclusion, Libby was informed he would be given a thirty-day trial as an observer.

Libby was posted to 23 Squadron, based at Le Hameau, ten miles west of the town of Arras; the unit had recently arrived from England in their F.E.2b two-seater biplanes. There were eighteen of the aircraft when Libby arrived at the aerodrome, which appeared to him to be nothing more than an abandoned field with nine canvas hangars. Once the introductions were over, Libby was asked what he knew about machine-guns. As little as knew about airplanes, he replied. Libby was given half an hour's shooting on the firing range with a Lewis gun. When he returned an F.E.2b was waiting for him on the runway, piloted by Lt. Stephen Price. Libby was horrified, not only at the prospect of going up in the air for some target practice but at the "ship" before him.

The F.E.2b was known as a "pusher" aircraft: the engine was at the back, "pushing" the machine. Aircraft with their engines in front were known as "tractors" because they and the propeller pulled the machine through the air. "Pusher" aircraft had a reputation for stability and for excel-

Captain Stephen Price was so impressed with Libby's sharpshooting as an observer in F.E.2bs that he took the American with him when he became commander of 11 Squadron in 1916.

lent visibility, and the enormous engine to the rear of the pilot and observer offered a measure of protection from the bullets of a surprise attack from behind. But the aircraft also had a couple of deadly drawbacks. Any loose object—such as an ammunition drum or a map case—could easily be sucked into the rear-mounted propeller in mid-flight, with fatal consequences. And if the F.E.2b was forced to crash land, the chances of survival were slim. Far more likely both the pilot and observer would be crushed to death by the engine.

Libby was 5 feet 9 inches tall, so not a particularly small man, which caused him some problems, as he explained in a letter:

> The pilot was in front of the motor in the middle of the ship and the observer in front of the pilot. When you stood up to shoot [in the F.E.2b], all of you from the knees up was exposed to the elements. There was no belt to hold you. Only your grip on the gun and the sides of the nacelle stood between you and eternity. Toward the front of the nacelle was a hollow steel rod with a swivel mount to which the gun was anchored. This gun covered a huge field of fire forward. Between the observer and the pilot a second gun was mounted, for firing over the F.E.2b's upper wing to protect the aircraft from rear attack. . . . Adjusting and shooting this gun required that you stand right up out of the nacelle with your feet on the nacelle coaming [*sic*]. You had nothing to worry about except being blown out of the aircraft by the blast of air or tossed out bodily if the pilot made a wrong move. There were no parachutes and no belts. No wonder they needed observers.

Libby judged his first flight a disaster. At the first pass, the goggle-less Libby couldn't even see the target (a large gasoline tin) because his eyes were streaming from the rush of wind; on the second pass, he fired the entire forty-seven-round drum from the Lewis gun, hitting the tin, but losing the empty drum as he replenished his ammunition. The discarded drum narrowly missed both the head of Lieutenant Price and the propeller, and Libby returned to earth crestfallen.

However, the British were delighted. The fact he had hit the target was a bonus, they told the American, but his greatest accomplishment was in firing at all. "I have seen them freeze and never shoot," said Chapman, the gunnery sergeant. "Shooting from the air, where you are all exposed, with nothing but your gun to keep you steady, is why so many men fail as observers."

Libby was given twenty-four hours to learn as much as he could about identifying enemy aircraft—how to tell if the small silhouette in the distance was a German Fokker or Albatros, a French Nieuport, or one of their own Bristol scouts." The pilot to whom he was assigned, Lt. Ernest Hicks, formerly a postal inspector from Winnipeg, offered some advice to Libby:

The rear gun is to keep Fritz off your tail when returning home from across the lines, when you can't turn and fight with the front gun. If this happens, you lose your formation back of the lines and have to fight your way home alone. This is tough and is just what the Hun is after. A lone ship they all jump on, so we try to keep formation at any cost if possible. Fighting your way home in a single ship, the odds are all in favor of your enemy. The wind is almost always against you because it blows from the west off the sea—this they know and they can wait. . . . [S]hoot at anything you see and don't know.

Libby learned quickly, but he was also a natural. "Aerial gunnery is ninety percent instinct and ten percent aim," he wrote in a letter, proving it on July 15, 1916 when, on a patrol with Hicks, he shot down his first enemy aircraft.

Such was Libby's prowess that when Lieutenant Price was promoted captain and appointed a flight commander of 11 Squadron—also stationed at Le Hameau—he took the American with him. On August 22, Libby was given credit for shooting down three

Though the British Bristol M.1C was powerful, the Air Ministry didn't trust it because it was a monoplane.

The observer's half wing was looked down on by some pilots, but great courage was required to perform the unenviable role. This observer, R. C. Dunn, fell to Manfred von Richthofen in 1917.

LFG Roland C.IIs, reconnaissance aircraft that like Libby's own "ship" comprised a pilot and observer. "Two bursts and he is upside down, then into a spin," wrote Libby of one victim. "I thought Price would jump out of our ship he was so happy."

Three days later, August 25, Libby shot down another aircraft, this an observation machine called an Aviatik C. He had now downed five aircraft, the number that qualified a pilot for "ace" status. But observers didn't receive the credit bestowed on fighter pilots. They were very much the poor relation within the RFC. Another American observer in the RFC, Arch Whitehouse, recalled the occasion in 1917 when he asked squadron orderly if there were any special insignia for his tunic.

"When you've done your first fifty hours over the line—and you pass all your ground tests—you get your wings. Then perhaps you'll be sent home to England for a commission and pilot training."

"A commission?" I positively glowed.

"Perhaps, that is," he added cautiously. "Anyway, you get your wing. It's a single-wing idea with an 'O' at the bottom." He leaned over again and whispered: "'Ere, we call it the flying arse-hole."[11]

Most observers, however, referred to themselves as P.B.O.s—Poor Bloody Observers—who performed the most dangerous job in the RFC. Nonetheless when they sewed the "flying arse-hole" on to the left breast of their tunic there was a feeling of overwhelming fulfillment.

[11] Arch Whitehouse, *The Fledging*

"This wing I shall always be proud of," wrote Libby when the time came for him to pick up the needle and thread. "When I think of all the observers who have 'gone west'[died] that were flying when I started, I have indeed been awfully lucky."[12]

Luck had played a part in Libby's survival—luck in having a pilot as skilled and calm as Captain Price—but his aggressive instincts were also a factor. In tandem, the pair were a match for any foe. "We were greatly outnumbered by the enemy," wrote Libby of his first "dogfight." "Here I learn the true value of a cool, experienced pilot like Price, who is alert and able to maneuver so the observer can keep the front gun in action, as in a dogfight the back gun is useless for the quick action necessary to keep the enemy from shooting you loose from your tail."

On September 26, Libby, by now commissioned as a second lieutenant, was awarded the Military Cross, one of the most prestigious gallantry medals in the British military. "As an observer, he with his pilot attacked 4 hostile machines and shot one down," ran the citation. "He has previously shot down 4 enemy machines."

In November 1916, Libby left France for England, and the School of Aeronautics, where for several months he learned to be a pilot and also collected his Military Cross from King George V at Buckingham Palace. For a cowboy from Colorado, the pomp and ceremony of the British monarchy was bewildering. Everywhere Libby looked in the palace were men in white wigs, boys in bright uniforms, and ornaments that dazzled. Luckily he had Stephen Price for support, also there to have a medal pinned on his chest. "He seemed very tired," Libby wrote of the king. "This damned war must be hell for him."

The ceremony over, Price and Libby left the palace and were photographed outside by the British press, all eager to make the most of the American cowboy who had just met the British monarch. Also waiting for Libby was Walter Hines Page, U.S. Ambassador to the United Kingdom, with an invitation to dine at the Embassy.

Libby returned to France in late April 1917, joining 43 Squadron who were flying Sopwith 1½ Strutters, a two-seater aircraft that, despite its rotary 130-horsepower engine, was easy prey for the German Albatros D.I fighters.

---

[12] According to Fred Libby, he required one hundred hours of flying time to qualify for the half wing.

Libby's presence was badly needed in 43 Squadron; that month, "Bloody April," they had suffered thirty-five casualties. Morale was low but Libby lifted the spirits with his reputation and his accent. "Everyone is kidding me now that America has declared war on Germany with good natured jibes such as 'How did you get here so soon?'" he wrote.

On May 6, Libby claimed his first kill as a pilot, "by simply pulling up the nose and pressing the control" of the front-facing Vickers machine gun. By the end of the month he was an acting flight commander, and in possession of a Stars and Stripes, a gift from a fellow officer who bought the flag while on leave in London.

As a flight commander, Libby was required to tie two colored ribbons, called streamers, to the struts of his aircraft to denote his rank (the second in command tied one streamer). Major Alan Dore, the squadron C.O., "upon seeing the flag, suggested I use it as a streamer or streamers just to show the Hun that America had a flyer in action." Libby cut the flag into two streamers and on May 28 flew with them on a patrol over German lines, continuing to do so for the rest of the summer.

He added three more victories to his total in the following months—the last two as a captain and flight commander in 25 Squadron—to take his tally to fourteen by the end of the summer of 1917. Then in early September Libby was told he was going home to the United States, whether he liked it or not. He was needed to train up America's novice aviators.

Libby's arrival back home after three years overseas was a disorienting experience for a young man still only twenty-five years of age. Having encountered the prurience of his relatives and the envy of his superiors, Libby was confronted with the zeal of the public when he returned to New York after his ordeal in Washington. After agreeing to auction his Stars and Stripes streamers to raise money for the Liberty war bonds drive, Libby was the center of attention when the auction was held on the steps of Carnegie Hall. His streamers were the second item on the bidding list, after the ribbon from a French Legion of Honor. That went for a six-figure sum prompting the auctioneer to announce as he unfurled Libby's streamers: "If the cordon of the French Legion of Honor is worth a million dollars, how much is Old Glory worth?" Bidding was ferocious, with the New York police department, the American Exchange National Bank, and silent movie actor William Farnum among those vying for the potent symbol of the American spirit. Eventually the flag

The American flag carried into battle by Fred Libby sold for a staggering $3,250,000 during an auction at Carnegie Hall in New York. *Library of Congress*

was sold to The National Bank of Commerce, for the staggering sum of $3,250,000.

The *New York Tribune* described the scene outside Carnegie Hall:

> A timid young officer with a tattered thing in his hand mounted the Liberty Theater platform yesterday, and while he stood there, cheeks burning with embarrassed red and eyes looking straight down his nose, a crowd that the moment before had gaped and grinned and jostled, after one slow stare, stormed toward him with sudden passion. They rolled forward in a tumult of noise, men and women with welcome in their voices and tears in their eyes—not Fifth Avenue sightseers cheering a show but a people greeting their own hero. . . . The first American flag to fly over the German lines, in the hands of the aviator who carried it there, had come back to New York to be baptized with the tears and kisses of a motley New York throng. Those hundreds sought to grasp the precious stripes of red and white and to shake the hand of Capt. Frederick Libby. This torn old thing,

amid all the bright flags of Fifth Avenue, was a holy banner and so the procession passed along, touching a rag as though performing a sacrament. Some touched it lightly. Some shook it lightly, some shook it as if it were a paw. The women kissed it, the soldiers saluted it, while Captain Libby still tried to hide behind it with the shame that any real hero seems to have for their own valor.

CHAPTER 4

Aren't We Ever Going to Fly?

In the same week of November 1917 that Fred Libby was facing up to life as a reluctant hero, John McGavock Grider told his diary of a visit to Oxford from a veteran officer of the RFC. "This individual hero stuff is all tommy rot," he told the Americans in an address. "It's devotion to duty and concerted effort and disciplined team work that will win the war."

The major then said that, by coming to England, the 150 aviators had taken the first steps on a long journey:

> It's a hard trip and will require a lot of courage. You'll all be frightened many times but most of you will be able to conquer your fear and carry on. But if you find that fear has gotten the best of you and you can't stick it and you are beyond bucking up, don't go on and cause the death of brave men thru [sic] your failure. Quit where you are and try something else. Courage is needed above all else. If five of you meet five Huns and one of you is yellow and doesn't do his part and lets the others down, the four others will be killed thru the failure of the one and maybe that one himself.

A fortnight later, Grider, Callahan, and all the cadets save for the twenty chosen by Elliott Springs to attend flight school in Stamford relocated to Harroby camp in Grantham, Lincolnshire. Grider was unhappy not to have been selected by his friend. "I couldn't see why he wouldn't take Cal and me and I told him so," he wrote in his diary. "What's the use of having friends if you don't stick by them and do things for them?"

Grider admitted to his diary that he had a case of the "blues." Winter had arrived in England. The days were colder, the nights longer, and melancholy seeped into his thoughts. "I could close my eyes and see the old living room at Grider with a big fire burning and Goodlookin' [his pet name for his estranged wife] undressing John and George in front of it while I laid on the settee or the chaise lounge and read or smoked. I didn't know how good it all was or could have been."

His own mortality weighed on his mind also. "I do want to see the kids bad," Grider told his diary. "Because I don't really expect to go back."

For Clayton Knight, also dispatched to Grantham, the rupture with Springs was a source of concern for reasons other than friendship.

Awarded a DFC for his "dash and skill," Lloyd Hamilton was shot down and killed flying with 17th Aero Squadron in August 1918.

"For quite a while the pay [from the American Aviation Corps] never caught up with us . . . so we were in great money difficulties," he recalled years later. "But Springs, who had plenty, acted as banker for a while."

Harroby camp afforded less salubrious accommodation than Oxford, and the cadets were obliged to share huts—though each hut had a servant assigned to its occupants to clean and shine shoes. "Everyone is fed up," wrote Grider just five days after their arrival at Grantham. "Aren't we ever going to fly?" Bored and disillusioned, the cadets sought outlets for their energies, drinking more than was good for them, often swigging back port in their huts late at night.

Then, on November 17, the cadets at Grantham began to be posted to flying schools around

England. Grider and Larry Callahan were among five cadets sent to Thetford; Donald Poler, a twenty-one-year-old who had attended ground school at Cornell University in early 1917, was assigned to the Gosport School of Flying, and Lloyd Hamilton was ordered to Tadcaster in Yorkshire.

Hamilton, the only child of a Methodist minister from Troy, New York, was a student at the Harvard Business School when war with Germany was declared. In May 1917, he volunteered for the army before deciding, two months later, to join the fledging air service. According to the major in charge of the Tadcaster flying school, Hamilton proved "the best and most apt pupil" he'd seen.

In Gosport, on the south coast of England, Donald Poler soloed in five hours and twenty minutes. "It wasn't too good as some fellows got to solo at around three and a half hours," he recalled. Part of the challenge for Poler was familiarizing himself with the aircraft, the Avro 504, a two-seater biplane that was the RFC's preferred training machine. "The Avro was quite stable and very light on the controls," he said. "One could drop an Avro from twelve feet and it wouldn't do any harm." That was not always the case, as Poler discovered when he misjudged a landing one day: "The right wing crumpled, then the forward skid, the prop and engine went into the ground and I just lost four front teeth."

At Thetford the aspiring aviators learned to fly in the Maurice Farman MF.11 Shorthorn, a French-made light bomber that had become obsolete on the Western Front by 1915. Grider recoiled when introductions were made, telling his diary they "are awful looking buses. . . . I am surprised they fly at all."

But fly they did and by the first week of December Grider had soloed in one. With the psychological barrier breached, he set his heart on learning to master the single-seater scout and to become a fighter pilot. His first sight of a scout machine (as fighter aircraft were known) was of a Sopwith Pup, a docile and maneuverable aircraft that had been introduced by the RFC the previous year. "It's the prettiest little thing I ever laid my eyes on," he wrote. "I am going to fly one if I live long enough. They aren't as big as a minute and are as pretty and slick as a thoroughbred horse."

On December 16, George Vaughn wrote to inform his family that "Harold Bulkley and I have now about finished our time, and will probably be posted to some more advanced school before very long."

This Avro 504 has crashed to earth, but on the whole the aircraft was a tough, reliable machine. It was used initially for reconnaissance patrols and for bombing missions before becoming a favorite training aircraft of the RFC.

A week later, however, neither Vaughn nor Bulkley had been posted, and the pair spent much of the time eating, since bad weather precluded flying. Breakfast consisted of cereal with ham and eggs, "some kind of fish or sausages," toast, jam, and coffee; for lunch there was "some kind of meat," vegetables, and dessert; tea, an English tradition that was maintained despite the war, was taken between four and five o'clock, and comprised bread and butter, jam, cake, and tea. Finally, if the aviators were still hungry, at seven o'clock they could gorge on "either soup or fish, meat and vegetables, dessert, crackers and cheese, and coffee."

Elliott Springs was also dining well, writing to tell his parents on December 27 of a sumptuous Christmas dinner in London, eaten in the presence of Lt. Alex Matthews, an old classmate of his at the Culver Military Academy of Indiana, who had arrived in England a few weeks earlier to train with the RFC.

Springs had been returned to Stamford after his brief posting to 74 Squadron because of a bureaucratic blunder over his rank. Despite a request in October from the British, the American military had not officially commissioned Springs or his fellow aviators, so despite passing out from flying school, he was unable to take up a posting with a British squadron. "There's no telling when I'll get it," he told his father. "The censorship won't permit me to give my opinion of the way we've been handled [by the American Signal Corp] in that respect."

The somber mood at Stamford was deepened by a series of three fatal crashes in four days in December: the popular Harold Ainsworth from Philadelphia was one of the victims. He had been performing a series of loops over the aerodrome at four thousand feet when the wings broke up.

Springs decided to keep a diary for 1918. His first entry ran:

"1 January 1918. I began the New Year in the most approved manner. At the stroke of 12 [Robert] Kelly [a cowboy from Arizona who had come over on the *Carmania*] and I were lying most socially in the gutter being very binged. 1918, may you bring me at least an honorable demise."

The fun lasted more than a week. "We drink until I pass away," wrote Springs on January 9, after another night's drinking with Kelly. Then three days later he was assigned to the 56th Training Depot Station at London Colney. "Deep gloom here," he told his diary. There were only two Avros to train on there, but he was delighted to discover that Callahan and Grider had also been assigned to the depot.

Grider had some bad news to pass on to Springs—the death of another cadet, Joe Sharpe, who had given Grider such a good fight in the Oxford boxing tournament. "Poor fellow . . . nose-dived into the ground from 1,500 ft," Grider told Springs.

The specter of death made the cadets more appreciative of life, particularly the Three Musketeers, whose motto was "Live for the Moment." On January 15, Grider threw what Springs called a "big party." Unfortunately, the rest of his description in the diary entry is illegible. The following day the three friends, together with Robert Kelly and two other cadets, went to London and "endeavor [ed] to wreck the Savoy", one of the city's most exclusive hotels. On January 18 they were at it again, incurring the wrath of their commanding officer who "gives us hell." Additionally, a steady stream of attractive young women were making the trek north from London to St. Albans,

Fatal training accidents were common during the early phase of a pilot's career. *Library of Congress*

the nearest town to London Colney. On February 7, Grider told his diary about an adventure "with a charming, unsophisticated damsel in St Alban's." Her name was Madge and she was "pretty with eager big blue eyes and the reddest lips I ever saw." However, confessed Grider, "my conscience haunts me. Oh well, take the fruit the Gods provide."

None of this found its way into the letters Grider wrote his family. Around the same time he was making Madge's acquaintance, he told his sister: "We are sportsmen of leisure. We have two classes a day and fly a good deal. We rise at nine and retire at eleven. We have the best food in England and very comfortable quarters. We sleep on folding cots and carry our furniture with us when we go."

As for his flying, Grider described how he was "now learning the art of looping, spinning, turning side slips, tail slides, flat spins and vertical banks on the finest bus that ever was built for the purpose. If you get into trouble, all you have to do is put everything in neutral and she comes out in flying position herself. It's a rather queer feeling at first to look up and see the ground instead of looking down, but you get used to it soon and it's the greatest sport there is!"

To his diary, Grider was again more honest. On February 8, Fred Stillman Jr., a 6-foot-7-inch-tall athlete who "used to play end on Yale" collided with another Avro three thousand feet above the aerodrome at London Colney. One of the fuel tanks erupted and the two machines fell to earth locked in a fiery embrace.

George Vaughn and his good friend Harold Bulkley were posted to 85 Squadron at Hounslow aerodrome[13] early in the New Year of 1918. It was a good spot to be, within easy access of the center of London thanks to the Underground trains. Fog grounded the pilots for much of January, so Vaughn and Bulkley rode the subway to London where they shopped, dined, and took in matinees at one of the West End theatres.

On Sunday February 17, Vaughn wrote his family that they were still awaiting their commissions from the American Signal Corps but they were rumored to be "getting nearer and nearer." He also described how he and Bulkley had been caught up in a German air raid the previous night as they dined out in central London. "We spent the rest of the evening in the 'Tube' station, waiting for the all-clear," he wrote, adding with an airman's disdain: "It was a very weak attempt at a raid, as a matter of fact." Vaughn ended the letter by telling his folks he had to go to bed as he had to be at the aerodrome early next morning for his "first trip" in a single-seater scout "which does well over a hundred miles an hour."

The machine in question was a Sopwith Pup, an aircraft that Bulkley, but not Vaughn, had already flown. Bulkley took the Pup for a short spin and then landed. It was Vaughn's turn. Bulkley, meanwhile was told by Captain Dell Clark to take up an Avro. The weather was good so why not make the most of it before the fog reappeared?

There were a number of aircraft in the sky over Hounslow on the morning of February 18, and more were waiting on the ground to take off. As Bulkley glided in to land he noticed "a large machine in the middle of the aerodrome." Believing he hadn't enough room to land, Bulkley switched on his engine and his aircraft rose sharply to the right, smashing into the undercarriage of another aircraft whose pilot also had an eye on the large machine below. The impact buckled the wings of Bulkey's aircraft, and, like a crippled bird, he dropped out of the sky.

[13] Now the site of Heathrow International airport

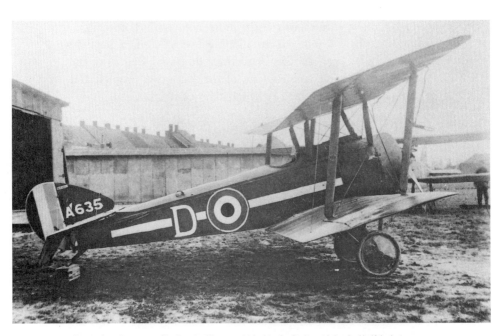

More agile and maneuverable than the Albatros at high altitude, the Sopwith Pup had half the horsepower of its German rival and also carried just one .303-inch Vickers machine gun. This Pup of 54 squadron was shot down in October 1917.

The sad task of organizing the return of his friend's personal effects to his family in New Jersey fell to Vaughn. He also cabled his parents and asked them to notify Mr. and Mrs. Bulkley of their tragic loss. Four days later Vaughn was one of the pall-bearers as Bulkley was laid to rest in Heston churchyard, the coffin draped in an American flag and conveyed on a gun-carriage.

The next day Vaughn received word from the American Aviation Section, whose headquarters were in Eaton Place, London, that his commission had arrived and would be sent on to Hounslow. Bulkey's commission was also being forwarded there.

CHAPTER 5

The Cream of the Cadets

In the same week of February 1918 that Harold Bulkley was buried, Elliott Springs wrote his father from his quarters at London Colney. "The Three Musketeers have extinguished themselves again in high society. Yes, we went raspazassin the other night—Callahan, Grider and myself—and not since the days of Oxford did we burst forth with such glory."

Springs's father had no idea what his son was talking about. "Raspazassin"? What the hell was that? Springs explained. A "real raspazas affair" was different from "snaking," the Musketeers' other favorite pastime—save for flying. "Snaking" was accepting a dinner invitation from a well-to-do English family in which one was wined and dined, and in return the Musketeers told the lady of the house "all about flying and why it isn't like riding an elevator." The result? "You get another free meal and if you're good at it you sort of get to be a member of the family and drop in without invitation."

But raspazassing was different. "Say we're out snaking and our hostess has Lady Agatha to dinner and Lady Agatha takes a fancy to us and invites us to dine with her next Thursday at a state dinner at eight and will send her car for us. Lord and Lady —— will be there as will the Hon Bertie and the Honorable Alice etc. No entertainment is expected of us—nor will be tolerated. For once the Americans will be overawed. Well, that is raspazassing."

The raspazassing that Springs was so keen to tell his father about concerned an invitation to a dinner in which the great and the good of English society appeared to have gathered. The dinner itself was "stiff" and formal; Callahan, Grider and Springs were all a bit overwhelmed by the amount of cutlery and the breadth of conversation.

Later, the the evening took a different turn. Grider, his inhibitions loosened by port, "got very sacrilegious trying to get the titles straightened out." So you're Lord X, and you're the Earl of Y, and the gentleman over there is the Duke of where?

The Englishmen found it hilarious, unaccustomed as they were to the Americans' merry irreverence to their standing in life. Once the port and cigars were finished, the gentlemen joined the ladies in the drawing room. One lady of impeccable breeding was sat at a piano playing what seemed to Springs like a dirge. "I lazed over to our hostess and told her that Cal [Callahan] could play some native American music," Springs told his father. "She asked him to and he made for the piano and sort of fingered it tenderly for a moment. Then he dug down into the insides of that instrument and extracted a rag such has never been heard before. The piano roared and swayed like a dozen Jazz bands and everybody began to look up and wiggle."

One of the Englishwomen squealed with delight, and grabbing Grider exclaimed: "Do show me how you Americans dance!"

Grider was only too happy to oblige, taking the hand of the "sweet young thing" and showing her how to dance ragtime. Others followed their lead and soon the drawing room was a dance floor as the English cast off their cloaks of reserve. "The party became a regular cabaret," Springs told his father. "One of the Englishmen did a burlesque drill with a German musket (captured at Ypres) and Mac [Grider] had to sing the Blues four times before they'd let him stop. Somebody played the piccolo and the flunkeys simply panted from their labors."

On February 15, the roistering came to a temporary end when some of the Americans were posted to gunnery school in Scotland. The qualification for gunnery school was the completion of twelve hours of flying time in a "service type" machine—the sort of aircraft the student would fly once posted to a combat squadron.

Springs and Callahan filled the criterion and travelled north to Turnberry, a small coastal town fifty miles southwest of Glasgow; Grider had yet to qualify. There, they were reunited with a number of other cadets from the *Carmania*, among them Lloyd Hamilton and

Donald Poler. Springs considered Turnberry to be a genteel, conservative town with no girls and no ragtime. "Everyone very snotty," he told his diary on February 16. Three days later, Springs wrote that Reed Landis had showed up in Turnberry.

Like Springs, the twenty-one-year-old Landis came from good stock. His father, Kenesaw Landis, was a federal judge who in 1920 would be appointed the first commissioner of baseball. Landis had served as a private in the Illinois National Guard on the Mexico border in 1916. One of the fifty-two cadets who sailed from New York on RMS *Aurania* in August 1917, Landis was a fine-looking young man with strong features and slicked-back brown hair. But he brought to Turnberry bad tidings: Harold Bulkley and another cadet, Lindley DeGarmo—along with Elliott Springs, the first of the cadets to qualify for their commission—had been killed in flying accidents. The next day, February

The son of a federal judge, Reed Landis was among the original fifty-two cadets who sailed to England in August 1917 aboard RMS *Aurania*. He finished the war an ace with twelve kills.

20, came news of another fatal accident, the death of Donald Carlton who failed to come out of a practice spin. To lift the depression Lloyd Hamilton and three other cadets hosted a party. "Never have I seen a bunch drunker," wrote Springs.

For the rest of February, Springs and his compatriots flew regularly, usually west over the Irish Sea, where they practiced their gunnery. On February 27, the Americans graduated from the gunnery school and were sent a few miles up the west coast of Scotland to Ayr, and the No. 1 School of Aerial Fighting.

John McGavock Grider arrived at Turnberry just as Springs and Callahan were departing for Ayr. He informed his fellow Musketeers that Clark Nichol had been killed at Stamford during his first solo flight. Another of the *Carmania* crew was gone.

Arthur Taber had soloed for the first time on January 15, 1918. He was so excited about the momentous event that he wrote a long letter home elucidating why it had taken him so long to fly without an instructor. Firstly, there was the difference in aircraft control. Some of the Curtiss JN-4 biplanes came with a stick control, others with a Deperdussin control wheel. "It is like changing from a saddle-horse, which is bridle-wise, to one which is not," Taber explained. Then there were his instructors, five in total since he'd arrived in England. Each had a different way of coaching, said Taber:

> . . . and I had to adapt myself to the man I was flying with; for instance, one man would fly straight and level until he came abreast if a point he wanted to make, then he would throw the machine over on one wing until the planes were nearly vertical, whirl about and flatten out again (he had been on scouts at the front); another man would make a wide and gradually sweeping turn (he had been on night bombing); another would make a moderately sharp turn, something between the two extremes, and would want me to do likewise. There is one more causing for the delay in my getting off, and that is that the eight hours of [dual] instruction were spread out over such a long period, one forgets during the interval between flights, and loses the knack.

It was a sorry litany of excuses for his own ineptitude as a pilot. The truth was that while the rest of his Oxford classmates had long since became proficient aviators, Taber was still struggling to master the basics. But at least he was alive. He owed that to his innate sense of caution, that once he was in the air verged on timidity. While Vaughn, Hamilton, and the Three Musketeers got a kick out of looping the loop and putting their "ships" into vertical spins, Taber found merely flying in a straight line a challenge. "As you fly along with the machine under complete control, you wonder what could possibly happen, and feel as safe as can be, even making allowances for the motor's failing," he wrote his father on January 24. "This is the time to look out for, and it is at just such as this time that good pilots are caught napping." Taber ended his letter with a reassurance for his father: "The exercise of prudence and common sense will see you through all right, and I am putting these convictions into practice."

Taber's timidity hadn't escaped the attention of his British instructors. They had no use for someone of Taber's docility so they didn't even bother to send him to Scotland to learn how to become a fighter pilot. Instead, they asked the Americans to take him off their hands. In February, Taber was sent over the Channel to join the American Expeditionary Forces' 3rd Air Instructional Center in Issoudun, central France. On one of his several jaunts into Paris, Taber ran into an acquaintance from the States and complained that "he had not had enough to do in the English camp or here in France."

In contrast, George Vaughn had impressed his British instructors so much that by the first week of March 1918, he was deemed ready to make the transition from Sopwith Pup to the S.E.5 (Scout Experimental 5). A single-seater biplane, the S.E.5 had entered service in April 1917 and proved itself fast—it could reach 132 miles per hour at 6,500 feet—and sturdy, if a little lacking in maneuverability, with its power provided by a new water-cooled 150-horsepower Hispano-Suiza 8 engine. Soon, however, the engine got a reputation for unreliability because of its gear reduction system problems, so a 200-horsepower Wolseley Viper engine was fitted. Elliott Springs also got to fly the machine in the spring of 1918 and recalled that "it would climb at 1,800 RPM to 20,000 feet in about thirty minutes." As for its armaments, the S.E.5 had two guns—"a Vickers firing through the prop[eller] and a Lewis on the top wing."

On March 9 Vaughn went to American headquarters in London to collect his commission, only to discover that it, along with those of all the other cadets, had come through as a second lieutenant and

The flying field at Issoudun, central France, where Arthur Taber spent much of his time. *Smithsonian Institution*

not a first. "Ours should be along very soon now," he told his family. "Just as soon as they can get it straightened out in Washington." The correct commission arrived a day or so later, along with confirmation that, as an officer, he would receive $185 a month. Glowing with pride, Vaughn completed his twelve hours of flying time on the S.E.5 and headed north to the Gunnery school.

He arrived in Turnberry just as John McGavock Grider finished his own gunnery course and departed for Ayr. "Your little Bud is now a graduate pilot," he wrote his sister. "I can fly any old thing they build; I can't fly very well yet, but I can fly safely. I have passed the crashing stage. I think I am pretty lucky, too; ten of our boys 'went west' [an RFC euphemism for death] in training, and not over seven or eight of the two hundred are through yet. I expect my commission to arrive in about two weeks. I was recommended five weeks ago so it should be coming along any day now."

Grider likened his time at gunnery school to "teaching a boxer all sorts of funny side steps and counters, and then teaching him how to use them." All in all, Grider's prose glittered with contentment, and not for one minute did he regret leaving the plantation

The S.E.5 entered service in April 1917 and proved itself fast and sturdy. It carried a Vickers that fired through the propeller and a Lewis gun on the top wing.

behind. Their shared experience had made the cadets "real friends," explained Grider, and Scotland he described as "a wonderful place."

Springs was pleased to see Grider walk through the door at Ayr. Though he wasn't short on self-confidence, Springs derived a comfort from Grider's presence that he found hard to articulate. It might have been the fact that Grider was older, more worldly-wise, and in a way, the big brother he had never had. Grider came from a loving family, but Springs had lost his mother when he was young and was at constant war with his controlling father. With Grider, Springs could broach subjects that he never could with his father.

The first thing Springs told Grider when he arrived at Ayr was the death in training of Cushman Nathan, "a fine fellow, a very good friend of mine and an excellent pilot." Nathan was the second of Springs's roommates to die in a month, the first being Lindley DeGarmo. That night the Three Musketeers went out on the town together to drink to the memory of Nathan.

On March 25, Springs, Callahan, and Grider travelled south to London to meet Maj. Billy Bishop, a twenty-four-year-old Canadian who had just returned from a triumphant tour of his homeland. Bishop was the RFC's most successful fighter pilot. Holder of Britain's highest military honor, the Victoria Cross (VC), and slayer of fifty enemy aircraft, Bishop was second only to France's René Fonck and the great Manfred von Richthofen in the list of wartime "aces."

Not everyone liked Bishop, particularly some of his fellow pilots who had noted that more than a few of Bishop's "kills" were uncorroborated. Even his VC was shrouded in suspicion with no witnesses to his claim that he had swooped single-handedly on a German airfield and destroyed three aircraft as they prepared to take-off. Protocol demanded that for a VC to be awarded there must be witnesses, but, in this case, there appeared to be none, just the bullish claims of Bishop, a man who didn't share the reticence of many of his RFC comrades.

However, by late 1917, the British Empire was in need of clean-living heroes and Bishop fitted the bill. He was shipped off to Canada where he married his sweetheart, Margaret Eaton Burden, daughter of a business magnate, in the celebrity wedding of the year. Bishop also wrote his memoirs, *Winged Warfare*, a thrilling account of life as an ace. "It is great fun to fly very low along the German trenches and give them a burst of machine-gun bullets as a greeting in the morning,

French pilot René Fonck was the leading Allied ace with seventy-five victories, second only to Manfred von Richthofen overall.

or a good-night salute in the evening," he wrote. "They don't like it a bit, we love it. We love to see the Kaiser's proud Prussians running for cover like so many rats."

Such drivel only further antagonized Bishop's comrades. Everyone in the RFC feared low-level strafing above all else and no one found it "fun." As one pilot wrote home after reading the book: "There's no doubt that he's one of the best pilots that ever climbed into a machine, but writing about it and telling how I did this and I did that isn't considered too good form out here."

But the Three Musketeers were in awe of Bishop when summoned to see him in London. Upon his return to England, the Canadian had been given command of a newly-formed fighter squadron, No. 85, flying S.E.5s, and free rein to handpick his pilots. Many of those he chose he had flown with the previous year but he was also on the lookout for fresh talent, particularly from his own part of the world. One of the men selected as a flight commander by Bishop was Captain Spencer Horn, one of the senior instructors at Ayr, and an ace in Bishop's previous squadron, No. 60. Horn's father, William, was an Australian mining magnate and politician who had refused a knighthood because he objected to "titular distinction being made a matter of diplomacy, personal influence and barter."

Horn told Bishop that he might want to have a look at some of the American cadets now that they were all fully qualified. Specifically Horn mentioned Springs, Grider, and Callahan. Bishop summoned them to London and found Horn hadn't been wrong, saying later, "I knew cream when I saw it." But when the British approached the Americans for permission to have the men sent to 85 Squadron they were knocked back; the Americans also recognized "cream" and wanted the trio for themselves.

On March 27, Springs and his two friends sat glum-faced on the train heading north. "Back to Ayr after spending a day trying to fix it up to go overseas with Bishop," he wrote in his diary. "It can't be done. He's certainly a Prince."

The son of an Australian mining magnate and politician, Spencer Horn recommended Springs, Grider, and Callahan to Billy Bishop.

But Bishop wasn't the most famous flyer in the British Empire for nothing. Five days later, April 1, Springs told his diary: "Maj. Bishop intercedes. Capt. Horn and I throw a big party." The American Aviation Section Headquarters in London had relented and Bishop had his men.

Grider couldn't contain his excitement in a letter to his sister, Josephine. "Sis, I have glorious prospects of going over the lines with the fastest company in France," he wrote. "If I make the grade, my reputation is made; if I don't, why then I stand as good a chance as any of the other boys. I hope I make it, you will be proud of me if I do." In addition the Three Musketeers had also received their commissions. "Your brother's done good," exclaimed Grider, "and I am now a real honest-to-God officer!"

Captain Edwin Benbow was another of the aces handpicked by Billy Bishop for 85 Squadron in April 1918.

On April 7 the Three Musketeers moved into an apartment in one of the most exclusive addresses in London: Berkeley Square. Their landlord was Lord Athlumney, an Englishman typical of his generation and standing. A former Guards officer he was, recalled an associate, "a strict disciplinarian and at the same time radiated considerable bonhomie, allowing everybody to call him Jim." How the three Americans came to receive such an illustrious invitation is a puzzle, though perhaps his lordship was one of the aristocrats at the party earlier in the year when Callahan had played ragtime piano and Grider sang the blues.

In 1918, Lord Athlumney was the Army Provost Marshal of London, a man with an "unrivalled knowledge of life after dark" in the capital. It was common knowledge that he exploited his position by inviting "the ladies of the theatre to join the brethren of Athlumney Lodge after dinner and then to go on to a night club to complete the evening."

The day the Musketeers took up residence in Berkeley Square they had what Springs described in his diary as a "big housewarming party." Billy Bishop and his young bride were invited, as were Capt. Horn and Capt. Edwin Benbow, another ace handpicked for 85 Squadron. Among the women present were four sisters called Beard, and a dark-haired beauty from Kentucky, named Hallye Whatley, whose fragrant qualities couldn't mask the whiff of scandal that clung to her chiffon gowns. Estranged from her American husband, the twenty-three-year-old Whatley had come to London to spice up her life. She had succeeded spectacularly, with one contemporary newspaper describing her as "prominent in the liveliest set of fashionable society."

A week later, April 14, the Three Musketeers were joined by a number of their fellow American aviators for a party at the Elysee Hotel, close to Kensington Gardens, and within walking distance of Berkeley Square. It was a hell of a party. Grider manhandled a British officer trying to come between himself and his dancing partner, and only the intervention of Callahan saved the Englishman from serious damage. Springs, meanwhile, drank so much he lost the sight in his left eye for a couple of hours.

However, there was a reason for the excess—that is, if the Three Musketeers ever needed a reason. The next day several of the American cadets left for France to take up postings with fighter squadrons, among their number Bennett Oliver, Reed Landis, and Alex Matthews. They must have woken the following morning with more than just a sore head; probably a tight stomach would have accompanied the realization that they were finally on their way to the front line. They would have been aware, too, that the previous week Manfred von Richthofen, the Red Baron, had accounted for three more British pilots in two days, taking his tally to seventy-eight.

In his book, *Winged Warfare,* Bishop admitted the Baron was possessed of "undeniable skill," but had nonetheless endeavored to demean the great German ace with a story about the time in 1917 he and his fellow pilots had gone pig-hunting in France. A big fat sow had been caught, wrote Bishop, and "upon her we painted black crosses; a huge black cross on her nose, a little one on each ear and a large one on each side. Then on her back we painted Baron von Richthofen. So that the other pigs would recognize that she was indeed a leader, we tied a leader's streamer on her tail. This trailed for some three feet behind her as she walked."

If only the real Richthofen were so easy to catch.

CHAPTER 6

The Red Baron's Last Fight

April 1918 marked the first anniversary of Oliver LeBoutillier's combat initiation. "Boots," as he was better known, had been born in Montclair, New Jersey, in May 1894. Two days after he turned twenty-three he shot down his first German, an impressive feat for a young man who had made his first solo flight just ten months earlier.

LeBoutillier had been nine when the Wright brothers flew into history, an age when young boys are liable to become obsessed by the incredible. Thereafter he was fixated on learning to fly and, in 1916, he enrolled at the Mineola flying school on Long Island. "Win, lose or draw I had to be close to those old airplanes," he recalled. "There was a bi-plane with two propellers driven on bicycle chains, just like the original Wright aircraft. The engine was sat right in the center of the pilot and student, the pilot on the left side and the student on the right."

Four hours' instruction was all LeBoutillier had on the Wright Model B before his instructor, Howard Rinehart, said to him one morning in early July 1916: "Boots, it's very quiet, very swell, now you take off."[14]

---

[14] Beginning his flying career as an instructor at the Wright Brothers Flying School in Dayton, Rinehart subsequently became an aviation explorer, innovator, and manufacturer.

Oliver LeBoutillier, "Boots" to his buddies, was an American ace who witnessed the death of the Red Baron while flying with 209 Squadron.

So LeBoutillier took off, opening up the engine and listening to "these two big old propellers in the back clanking with these bicycle chains." He did a lap of the airfield, landed without too much problem, and became the 566th recipient of a *Fédération Aéronautique Internationale* license.

LeBoutillier returned to his family and showed them his license. They weren't too impressed, declaring he was "crazy" to want to fly. His father asked what he was going to do now with his life. "I want to fly," replied LeBoutillier, "and the only place I know is Canada."

His father was outraged and refused to pay his son's fare north. But his mother did, and when the American presented himself to the RFC in Ottawa, the British couldn't believe their luck. Here was a twenty-two-year-old in prime health, eager to fight, who was already a solo aviator, so there was no need to send him to the Curtiss Aviation School in Toronto. "They said I was just what they wanted," recalled LeBoutillier, who was sent immediately to England aboard "an old freighter" to join the Royal Naval Air Service (RNAS).

Two weeks later, LeBoutillier stepped off the ship and was directed toward the RNAS training facility at Crystal Palace, a few miles south of central London. Here "Boots" underwent his basic training and became acquainted with the ways of the Royal Navy. Time was measured in "bells" and the glass-structured palace was divided into decks as if it were a ship. To help him—and the dozens of Canadian recruits undergoing training—LeBoutillier was issued a handbook entitled *The Flyer's Guide* by Capt. N. J. Gill.

On the question of learning to fly, Captain Gill had this sanguine advice for the cadets: "If you look down, do it in a disinterested sort of way without wondering how hard you will hit the earth if something happens. It won't happen so why fill your head with rot of this kind? If you do feel that you are not quite happy, fight the feeling, and say to yourself 'it is all nonsense!'"

He also reminded them that "the word 'joystick' is never to be used in the Royal Naval Air Service." As for their behavior in public, cadets hardly needed reminder that jewelry of any sort was bad form for a man and for an officer in uniform was intolerable. In addition, "Officers should not smoke pipes in the street when in uniform." Finally, he had a word or two about etiquette in the mess: "Leave Senior Officers to themselves unless they show they want to talk to you. This is the best rule." And above all, "never mention a lady's name and do not use any form of swear word, or tell doubtful stories."

Once he had passed basic training, LeBoutillier was sent to Redcar, on the north-east coast of England, to learn how to fly Maurice Farman and French Caudron machines. The Caudron was a twin-engine biplane used, since its introduction the previous year, as a bomber. LeBoutillier crashed one on

Upon arriving in England in 1917, LeBoutillier was posted to the Royal Naval Air Service (RNAS), where pilots—such as this one—wore the blue of the navy, not the khaki of the RFC.

his first flight. Hauled up in front of the base commander, LeBoutillier expected to be returned to the United States in disgrace but the officer was "an old Englishman, very stern but very honest, and very careful about screening students. . . . [H]e knew it wasn't my fault, that the instructor had tried to push me too fast, so I got another instructor and another chance at flying, and then I did pretty good from then on."

At the start of 1917, LeBoutillier was sent down south to Dover, the nearest point in England to France, just nineteen miles across the English Channel. The historic town with its white cliffs was the "checkout point for pilots flying single seaters before they went to France." At Dover LeBoutillier was introduced to the Sopwith Camel, heralded as the superior version of the Sopwith Pup. Its armaments were indeed formidable; for the first time in a British-designed machine, two .303 Vickers machine guns were mounted directly in front of the cockpit with their synchronization gear enabling them to fire through the propeller disc. But that was one of the few positive points in the eyes of the men ordered to fly the Camel, which gained its name from the

The Sopwith Camel was well armed but unstable and got its nickname from the hump created by a metal fairing over the gun breeches designed to stop them freezing at altitude.

hump created by a metal fairing over the gun breeches to stop them freezing at altitude. Ninety percent of the Camel's weight was contained in the front seven feet of the aircraft—engine, fuel tank, pilot, and guns—so it was unstable and not anything like as maneuverable as the Pup.

In addition, the Camel's 150-horsepower Bentley rotary engines generated so much heat that ordinary engine oil proved useless. Instead, recalled LeBoutillier years later, they "used pure castor oil as lubricant." He continued: "At first it was pretty hard to get used to because when they start the engines the fumes came right back at you in the cockpit, and you're breathing castor oil the whole time. The castor oil gets into your flying suit and we smelled of castor oil all the time."

In April 1917 LeBoutillier, now a sub lieutenant, was assigned to 9 Squadron, RNAS, despite the fact he had logged only twenty-nine hours of solo flight time. The British had identified in the young man from New Jersey the traits required for a fighter pilot. These, recalled LeBoutillier, were "a certain aggressiveness . . . [and] the boys who

In addition, the Camel's 150-horsepower Bentley rotary engines generated so much heat that ordinary engine oil proved useless. They resorted to pure castor oil as lubricant, which created terrible fumes.

seemed to be the best fighter pilots were the ones that had done things the hard way; they didn't phase out when the odds were against them. They knew how to cope with it."

The task of 9 Squadron in the early summer of 1917 was to intercept German bomber squadrons bound for southern England. Attacks had been increasing in intensity in the preceding months ever since the Germans began replacing Zeppelins with the twin-engine Gotha bomber. On May 25, a fleet of more than twenty Gothas attacked the Channel port of Folkestone, killing seventy-one civilians, including twenty-seven children. The British were incensed, but powerless to hit back against an aggressor whose distant cities were beyond the reach of their own aircraft.

The next day the Germans came again, this time with a fleet of LVG (*Luftverkehrsgesellschaft*) bombers. However, they were intercepted by 9 Squadron over the Channel, and LeBoutillier claimed his first victim. Ten days later, he scored a second victory when his patrol encountered several Albatros scouts over the French coast waiting to escort a bombing mission to England. A third German fell to LeBoutillier's guns in July 1917, again an Albatros scout, which "turned on its back and went down out of control." At the end of the month "Boots" had four enemy aircraft to his credit.

By early 1918 LeBoutillier was one of 9 Squadron's veterans, a captain and the commander of B Flight. On April 1, the RNAS merged with the RFC to become the Royal Air Force [RAF]. No. 9 Squadron was reconstituted as 209 Squadron, and ordered to France to help repel the German ground offensive of March 21, a mass attack along the Western Front in which the Kaiser's army achieved the deepest advances by either side since 1914. It was the last throw of the dice for the Germans, an offensive aimed at defeating the British and French armies before the United States had the chance to bring its full weight to bear on the Western Front.

The arrival in France of 209 Squadron increased the RAF presence to sixty-three squadrons (an increase of eleven squadrons in four months thanks in no small part to the arrival of aviators from North America, Australasia, and South Africa) but of its 1,232 aircraft on the Western Front, only 580 were ready for combat at the point of attack, compared to 750 enemy machines.

LeBoutillier's squadron was one of several based at Bertangles, close to the Amiens-Albert road, about ten miles west of the front line, while "the Germans and Richthofen were stationed in a little

One of LeBoutillier's early tasks was to shoot down the twin-engine Gotha bombers that replaced Zeppelins as the primary aerial threat to Britain. On one raid on the Channel port of Folkestone in May 1917, a squadron of Gothas killed seventy-one civilians, including twenty-seven children.

LeBoutillier's first kill was an LGV (*Luftverkehrsgesellschaft*) bomber in May 1917.

place called Cappy, I'd say approximately the same distance on the other side of the German line."

LeBoutillier's respect for the Red Baron ran deep, and, like most RAF pilots, he knew much about his opponent. Unlike the British, as reluctant as ever to turn their top pilots into celebrities, the French and Germans had from the outset acclaimed the feats of their "aces." Neither nation shared the British concern that by creating a hierarchy among pilots they might damage the delicate camaraderie within a squadron; might not some of these ardent young men be tempted to go glory-hunting in the hope of joining the exalted ranks of the aces; to stray from the flight formation in the pursuit of fame rather than the foe?

In 1917 Richthofen wrote his autobiography, *Der rote Kampfflieger* (translated into English the following year), and Germans hung on his utterances, however bland or inconsequential. Americans, too, were transfixed by the Baron. On April 30, 1917, Ohio's *Lancaster Daily Eagle* was one of several newspapers to laud Richthofen, describing their enemy as "brilliant and daring." From the newspaper's breathless prose one wouldn't have guessed that their country had declared war on Richthofen and his comrades less than a month earlier. The Red Baron had just been awarded the *Pour le Mérite*, German's highest military medal (also known by the more informal moniker Blue Max on account of its color) by his Kaiser and the *Daily Eagle* told its readers: "He is the youngest man ever to receive this distinction, being twenty four years old. Von Richthofen shot down his fortieth enemy airplane, winning three air victories in a single day (on April 13, 1917)."

Six months later, in November 1917, the *Kansas City Star* carried the comments of Richthofen concerning the "reported preparation to place twenty thousand American aviators on the western front." It was his opinion that these inexperienced pilots will "be unable to judge the military conditions and at least twenty-five per cent of the machines will be disabled during the long transport."

In LeBoutillier's opinion, Richthofen had amassed so many kills because of his sharpshooting skills. "When he was a young fellow they gave him a gun and he'd go out and shoot the upland birds," he said. "He knew how to lead the birds so that stood him in good stead when it came to combat. . . . [H]is ability to lead and shoot a moving target. He had that one thing going for him."

The Baron shot down his seventy-eighth machine on April 7, 1918, but then, recalled LeBoutillier, the weather closed in and for several days "we had heavy clouds." For thirteen days Richthofen was unable to add to his tally but, on Saturday, April 20, the weather was fine and he bagged two more victims, both Sopwith Camels belonging to 3 Squadron.

The second of the two Camels was flown by a nineteen-year-old Rhodesian called Tommy Lewis, a rookie in combat who was easy meat for the Baron's bright red Fokker triplane. His emergency fuel tank ablaze, Lewis found himself "hurtling earthward in flames." His machine hit the ground at around 60 miles per hour, but miraculously the teenage flyer was catapulted clear suffering nothing more than a few minor burns. LeBoutillier heard later that "Richthofen came over while he was brushing the fire off his flying suit and waved to him. Tommy Lewis waved back."

When dawn broke on Sunday April 21, a mist was draped over the Somme valley. The pilots of 209 Squadron had breakfast and waited for it to clear. The tension was palpable. "We knew things were going to be pretty tough that day," said LeBoutillier. A few days earlier word had reached the squadron that "Richthofen's squadron was getting pretty upset with 209 and they wanted to try and wash them out."[15]

Although 209 Squadron had only been recently posted to France, many of its pilots were veterans having flown countless offensive patrols against German bombers the previous year. LeBoutillier was in charge of B Flight; Captain Oliver Redgate, an "ace," led C Flight; and Capt. Roy Brown was A Flight's commander. Brown was a twenty-four-year-old Canadian who had joined 9 Squadron in March 1917 and received the Distinguished Service Cross (DSC) later that year "for the excellent work he has done on active service."

The spring sunshine soon burned off the early morning mist and 209 Squadron began taking off, each of the three flights comprising five aircraft. "We had certain sectors to cover over the Somme River Valley along the front over the Morlancourt Ridge," recalled LeBoutillier. "Underneath was the Australian artillery."

Captain Roy Brown, the twenty-four-year-old Canadian of 209 Squadron, who many believe shot down the Red Baron in April 1918. Others believe it was ground fire from Australian infantry that downed Germany's top ace.

[15] *Jagdgeschwader* I, also known as the "Flying Circus," comprised *Jastas* 4, 6, 10, and 11.

At about the same time as 209 Squadron embarked upon their morning patrol, Richthofen and his pilots were climbing into their Fokkers twenty miles to the east, their gaudy colors a striking contrast to the vernal French countryside. The Baron was wrapped up well in his woolen flying jacket and deerskin trousers, the *Pour le Mérite* cross around his neck.

Once airborne, LeBoutillier led his B Flight toward the southern end of their sector at a height of 15,000 feet. "Brown was a little to the north and Redgate more or less center," recalled the American. "I was sent south because they said there were enemy aircraft there we should take out. . . . [W]e took out one." LeBoutillier, together with Lt. Robert Foster, shot down an Albatros two-seater in flames over Beaucourt but then "everything broke to the north of us."

LeBoutillier estimated that it took his flight three minutes to fly north, a lifetime in aerial combat. By the time he and his four Sopwith Camels arrived, the pilots of 209 Squadron were fighting for their lives against Richthofen's Circus. Frank Mellersh of A Flight had shot down a Fokker while Canadian Bill MacKenzie had been wounded in a duel with a German. LeBoutillier recounted that already "we'd lost four of our planes" so 209 Squadron was down to eleven aircraft against twenty-eight Germans.

"All you saw were Sopwiths and triplanes, all together," recalled LeBoutillier. "There were three or four red triplanes, but nobody knew Richthofen was in one of them." LeBoutillier opened fire on a Fokker but missed the target and "then one chased me for about twenty seconds. I pulled out to see if my wings were all shot up."

After shaking off his pursuer, LeBoutillier suddenly glimpsed "a pilot going under me with a red triplane after him." Only later would he learn the British pilot fleeing for life was Lt. Wilfrid May, a

Sunday, April 21, 1918, dawned cold and misty on the Western Front, and von Richthofen wrapped up warmly before what he assumed would be another day of rich pickings against his British opponents.

young Canadian from Manitoba who had joined the squadron a fort-night earlier. Brown had taken his compatriot under his wing and now saw the danger he was in. He joined the chase, hunting the triplane that was hunting May. LeBoutillier could tell it was Brown because of the streamers attached to his Sopwith. "He came down at a forty-five degree angle on the triplane and you could see the tracers going into the cockpit," recalled LeBoutillier. "Then he [Brown] pulled up into a climbing turn and he didn't see the red triplane again, and I didn't see Roy Brown again because I had my eyes on the triplane, which broke off from chasing May and at that time he started to make a great big gentle turn to the right."

LeBoutillier saw the triplane land in a field on a hill near the Bray-Corbie road. "He didn't hit too hard, hit on his wing-tip and right wheel and he hopped along the ground a little bit and stopped." LeBoutillier "came down, made a pass over, so I could go back and report it to the squadron." As he made his pass, the American noticed Australian soldiers on the ground.

They were the first to reach the downed triplane and to their amazement soon learned the identity of the pilot. Later that day word reached 209 Squadron that it had been the Red Baron himself in the

Instead of becoming the eighty-first victim of the Red Baron, Lt. Wilfrid May, a young Canadian from Manitoba, became known as the man who caused him a moment of fatal complacency.

downed triplane, the great man killed by a single bullet. The Australians claimed they'd fired the shot but that made no sense to LeBoutillier. "Richthofen had one bullet that went in his right shoulder at a forty-five-degree angle, that went through his body, at the same angle that Brown was firing at him," he reflected. "So they can say what they want about ground troops . . . but in my opinion von Richthofen was hit by Brown." The debate over who killed Richthofen continues to this day.

Von Richthofen's bright red Fokker triplane was swooped on by souvenir hunters, all eager for a piece of the legendary Red Baron. The pilot who had decorated his own quarters with trophies taken from his eighty victims was a mute witness to the desecration of his legendary aircraft. "Our mechanics went over there and cut a piece of fabric from von Richthofen's aircraft," remembered LeBoutillier. "And the eleven pilots in that combat fight signed it." Above the signatures someone wrote, "Piece of fabric from Baron von Richthofen's aircraft, shot down by Roy Brown."

CHAPTER 7

Love and War

On April 30, 1918, Elliott Springs wrote his stepmother from his residence in Berkeley Square. "I suppose you saw in the papers that von Richthofen, the famous German pilot, has been killed. Everyone says it's too bad he couldn't have been taken prisoner."

Death was never far away from Springs's daily life. Either he was reading about it, or witnessing it. In the first week of May he saw Clarence Fry, another of the Oxford cadets, killed, and a few days later another of that small band, Chester Pudrith, former captain of the Dartmouth football team, met a similar fate.

Springs and Callahan also had crashes, but they walked clear without serious injury. Grider had little sympathy. "The only reason you fools are alive is that hell is already packed with aviators," he told them. Of the Musketeers Grider was the inferior pilot of the three, but what he lacked in flair, he made up for in prudence. Four years older than Springs, and two years the senior of Callahan, he had shed his youthful impetuosity while his two friends still wore their immaturity like medals of honor. "I have a rather good record about busting [aircraft]," Grider wrote his family. "I have not strained a wire except that one wing tip."

Though in his diary Grider pondered his own mortality, in his letters home he wrote only words of cheerful assurance. "My boss [Billy Bishop] led a flight over the lines for five months and never lost a man," boasted Grider in a letter to his friend, Emma Cox. "He is going to lead me so I feel pretty safe. Besides, I want to come home and live at San Souci [his plantation] with sister and keep Grider exclusively as a road house for my friends."

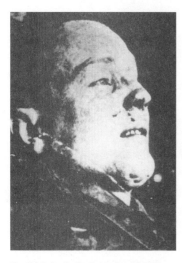

Von Richthofen dead at Bertangles airfield. The British subsequently buried him with full military honors.

Grider longed to tell his friends and family "about our squadron" but he knew such details would never pass the censor. Bishop, Benbow, and Horn must all remain secret, so too the squadron number, but Grider reassured his correspondents that the outfit was "the best and the three Musketeers are in it. I hope to God we will be out before long."

At the beginning of May, 85 Squadron was still at Hounslow, constantly training, but their mood brightened when they finally took delivery of their brand new S.E.5s. "I have been a child with a new toy ever since," Springs told his father on May 12. "I've been cleaning and oiling my machine guns, tuning up the motor, and testing the rigging continually."

Springs wanted to prove a point to his father, to show that he was now his match as a man, and was no longer a child to be patronized. "You ought to see the gadgets," he bragged of his aircraft's cockpit. "Compass, air speed indicator, radiator thermometer, oil pressure gauge, two gas pressure gauges, tachometer, compensator, two gun trigger controls, synchronized gear reservoir handle, hand pump, two switches, pressure control, wheel altimeter, gas pipe shut-off cocks, shutter control, thermometer, two cocking handles for the guns, booster magneto, spare ammunition drums, map case, throttle, joystick and rudder bar. How's that for something to keep your eye on?"

The description was designed to confound. There was no explanation as to what items such as a booster magneto might be. Springs must have chuckled as he imagined his father scratching his head in puzzlement. It was his way of telling him to stick to his nineteenth century cotton mills while he mastered the very latest in twentieth century technology. Springs customized his cockpit after the first couple of test flights, adding a cupboard and shelf for spare goggles, machine gun tools, cigarettes, chewing gum.[16]

---

[16] It wasn't uncommon for pilots to modify their aircraft. Reed Landis installed a half-inch-thick steel plate to the underside of his seat as protection against antiaircraft fire, while Frank Dixon recalled that on his Sopwith Camel the "guns and sights were at eye-level and a distinct hazard in a forced landing so I rigged up a plexiglas windshield and cut away the cowling to meet it."

"You know, when you're in the air for two or three hours at a time you get awfully bored." However, of course his father didn't know; the only thing he'd ever piloted was an automobile.

Larry Callahan wasn't quite so delighted with his machine on account of an engine he believed faulty. Together with his mechanics he looked it over. But at least he had an aircraft. Grider's S.E.5 had been smashed during its delivery when its ferry pilot ran into some telegraph wires attempting to land.

However, by now Grider had things on his mind other than flying. He was in love. In the six months since arriving in England, all three Musketeers had participated in what they called "horizontal refreshments" with some of the scores of young women who found pilots—particularly North American ones—as dashing as dashing could be. Springs's diary was littered with the names of women he'd seduced, while, on April 12, he described how Grider and Alex Matthews "fight over Sheila."

Then Grider met Billie Carleton. The exact date his eyes first fell on her isn't known. It was probably a meeting made possible through their acquaintance with Lord Athlumney. Perhaps the pair

Larry Callahan (left) and his other two Musketeers worshipped Canadian ace Billy Bishop (center), seen here with 85 Squadron.

met at one of his parties. But wherever they met, it was love at first sight for Grider.

If Springs wrote home with boyish excitement about his aircraft, Grider's adolescent boasting was induced by the twenty-two-year-old Carleton. To his friend Emma Cox he wrote:

Three of us—the Three Musketeers—are stationed in London, almost, and have been living in a house in Berkley square. Tell papa that none of us are the Tomlinsons by any means though the devil wouldn't hesitate a minute to take us into hell. Emma, at last I am having a real romance. I wish you could see the girl. The only trouble with is her salary. She gets £5,000 a year and has a very nice private income besides. She is one of the most sought after women in London and almost every evening I strut into the Carlton or the Ritz [two of London's most exclusive hotels] with this wonderful vision on my arm. All the women hate her and copy her clothes. Her name is Billie Carleton and she is on the stage playing "Fair and Warmer." Some girl. Emma, I do wish you could attend some of our parties. Honey, the youth and beauty of London are there, also the talent. . . . [W]e are going with the fastest, keenest crowd in London and I have gotten away with the handsomest, most charming and sought after girl in the drove. Some class![17]

But there was more to Billie Carleton than met the eye. Yes, she was beautiful, and yes, she was undoubtedly talented, an accomplished pianist, dancer, singer, and actress. Her first break had come in 1914 when the impresario C. B. Cochran promoted her from the chorus line to star in *Watch Your Step* at London's Empire Theatre. "Despite her inexperience and her tiny voice, she pleased the audiences," recalled Cochran. "A more beautiful creature has never fluttered upon a stage. She seemed scarcely human, so fragile was she."

But Carleton had inherited something other than musical talent from her parents—an addictive personality. Alcohol had been her father's weakness; hers was drugs. Early on during the run of *Watch Your Step*, word reached Cochran that Carleton was being "influenced by some undesirable people and was going to opium parties."

He sacked her from the role and her career teetered on the brink. If there hadn't been a war on Carleton might have slipped back into obscurity. But London in 1915 was a louche, decadent city, with more than 150 night clubs opening during the war years, and notoriety was to be celebrated, not stigmatized as it had in the pre-war years. A mysterious man called John Marsh, twenty years Carleton's senior,

[17] Ambrose Tomlinson founded the Church of God in Tennessee in 1903 and his children were similarly devout.

"You ought to see the gadgets!" Elliot Springs wrote his father after taking delivery of his first S.E.5a and peering inside the cockpit.

and said to be "the backbone of half a dozen big money-lending concerns," became her patron. He installed Carleton in a flat in Savoy Court Mansions, and it was he who provided the annual income of £5,000 that so impressed Grider. The money was managed by Frederick Stuart, a Knightsbridge physician, while another man she met through Marsh was Reggie de Veulle, a dress designer whose creations she modeled. Such generosity enabled Carleton to be seen in the best dresses in the best clubs with the best people. She was also able to feed her drug habit.

Carleton was far from alone in her addiction. In April 1916, "information reached the police and the authorities that a new and most pernicious habit had sprung up in the selling of cocaine in small quantities." Most of the users were soldiers on leave from the front, doubtless seeking an escape from the horrors they'd seen in the trenches. In May 1916, a law was passed by the British government "prohibiting the traffic" of cocaine but it did little to disrupt the flow of

John Grider fell head over heels in love with Billie Carleton, a stage beauty with an addictive personality. *From "The Freedom of the Seas,"* Play Pictorial, *July 1918*

drugs into London. In November 1917, "information was received by Scotland Yard that de Veulle was trafficking in cocaine with Billie Carleton."[18]

Carleton's stage career was booming once more at this point. Cochran had given Carleton a second chance and cast her in *Hoop-La* at the St. Martin's Theatre in November 1916, and the following year, she starred in *Some (More Samples!)*, prompting society magazine *Tatler* to predict "a very brilliant future for Miss Carleton in musical comedy."

However, as Carleton's fame grew, so did her addiction. One of the handsome young men in "her set" was Lionel Belcher, a film actor who had played the romantic lead in the 1917 movie *Another Girl's Shoes*. As impressionable as Carleton, but without her private income, his drug habit soon landed him in heavy debt. He therefore became a dealer to keep his creditors at bay. One evening he was at a party laden with cocaine when "the door opened and there entered, also in pajamas, the girl who was the idol of London."[19] Belcher recalled that: "I have rarely, if ever, seen a more beautiful woman than Billie Carleton. In addition to her wonderfully expressive eyes, which could melt appealingly or sparkle with vivacity and laughter, which were still at twenty-two those of a child of fifteen, her coloring was perfect. . . . [S]he was a woman to whom no man in the world could refuse anything."

On May 11, Carleton sent the Three Musketeers tickets for the opening night of *Fair and Warmer* at the Prince of Wales theatre. The farce had come to London from Broadway, and Springs told his father that "the English audience always laughed at the wrong time and their idea of American slang was simply weird."

Nonetheless it was worth going just to see Carleton. Springs was as in thrall to her beauty as Lionel Belcher had been. "Oh, la la, what a knockout!" he wrote of her following the first night party. "Billie and

---

[18] The *Syracuse Herald*, August 3, 1919

[19] The *San Antonio Light*, October 2, 1926

'Mac' Grider got on like Antony and Cleopatra. How that woman can dance! . . . She is about twenty-three and has been on the stage since she was eighteen. She sure is witty. She kept us laughing all evening."

After the party Grider escorted Carleton back to her flat in the Savoy Court Mansions where she "slipped into a negligee and looked like a million dollars." Fortunately for Grider, he was well versed in "horizontal refreshment," for Carleton was as racy as her image suggested. She frequented opium parties at the flat of de Veulle in Dover Street where, once dinner was finished, the male guests "divested themselves of their clothing and got into pyjamas, and the women into chiffon nightdresses." There then occurred "disgusting orgies" during which Miss Carleton "arrived later at the flat from the theatre, and she, after disrobing, took her place in this circle of degenerates."[20]

How much Grider knew of Carleton's private life is unclear. Given her propensity for cocaine, an open secret in London, it seems unlikely he was oblivious to her addiction. He probably ignored it, his eyes blinded by love.

Grider spent every spare minute in Carleton's company, and then one day he announced to Springs and Callahan that they were going to get married. "Larry and myself were rather worried about it," Springs wrote his stepmother. "Not that we weren't both in love with the lady ourselves but we still don't care to have the Three Musketeers mixed up in matrimony." Grider even applied for a marriage license but Carleton "had the good sense to refuse at the last moment." The truth was that Carleton wasn't in love with Grider; he was just something different, a welcome change from the foppish actors and listless artists that comprised her usual crowd of hangers-on. To her, Grider was "her cave man," and on their last night together she teased him about it during a party at the Musketeers' flat in Berkeley Square. It was another wild night. One of Carleton's girlfriends smashed an empty port bottle over Springs's head and "he was out for some time."

The next morning, May 22, the Three Musketeers left their Berkeley Square home for the final time. Billie Carleton and some of her theatrical friends accompanied them to Hounslow. They arrived to find quite a crowd had gathered. "I don't think there ever was a squadron that got the send off we did," wrote Springs. "Two

[20] The *Times* (London), December 14, 1918

The boys of 85 Squadron at London Colony in spring 1918. From left to right: Elliot Springs, Spencer Horn, John McGavock Grider, unknown, and Malcolm McGregor.

princesses, a couple of generals, several colonels and majors and the 'drome was simply covered with pink parasols."

If there were two members of the royal family present, Springs only mentioned one by name: Princess Marie Louise, a granddaughter of Queen Victoria and a first cousin of German Kaiser Wilhelm II. Grider also singled out Her Royal Highness when he wrote his sister of the day. "You should have seen our departure from England. There was the princess Marie Louise, who is a peach of an old lady. She is also the sister of King George and the godmother of the 85th squadron. I had tea with her that afternoon and enjoyed talking to her very much."

Springs garlanded Mrs. Bishop with orchids and marveled at her "stiff upper lip." She in turn begged the eighteen other pilots of 85 Squadron to "stick to the major and not let a Hun get on his tail."

The pilots said their last farewells. Grider and Carleton embraced, and she slipped into his hands a doll she'd had specially made for her lover. It wore a miniature replica of one of her evening gowns, the one Grider most admired, and its hair had been delicately clipped from Carleton's own head. Grider loved it. He called the doll "Billie 2" and installed it in the rear of his fuselage as his mascot.

The pilots climbed into their S.E.5s and took off in their well-rehearsed formation, Bishop "out front in the center and the three flights arranged in a V on each side and in back of him."

The weather over the Channel was perfect as the squadron left England and headed to France and to war. Springs appeared unconcerned by what lay ahead. Halfway across the sea, at a height of 8,000 feet, he motioned to Grider to come in close. "I flew up to his wing tip," recalled Grider, "and he took out his flask and drank my health."

CHAPTER 8

Dogfighting Days

By the end of April 1918 the great German offensive of the previous month had been stemmed by the Allies, but at a considerable cost. More than 300,000 Allied soldiers had been killed or wounded (German casualties were put at 350,000) and the British, in particular, were at the end of their tether. As American "doughboys" were rushed to the front to replace the shattered remnants of the British army, a similar manpower problem was affecting the RAF. When the German offensive began on March 21, the RAF had 1,232 aircraft on the Western Front; six weeks later, all but 200 had been destroyed or damaged beyond repair.

Casualties were high because the war in the air, as on the ground, had evolved. The static trench warfare of the previous three years had given way to fluid fighting, the Germans penetrating as far as forty miles in some sectors of the Western Front. There hadn't been territorial advances like it since 1914, yet despite all their gains the Germans failed to make the decisive breakthrough.

The role of the RAF in the spring offensive had been significant. On April 11, 1918, Field Marshal Sir Douglas Haig, the Commander-in-Chief of the British Army, had issued his famous communique that passed into legend as his "Backs to the Wall" order:

> Three weeks ago to-day the enemy began his terrific attacks against us on a fifty-mile front. His objects are to separate us from the French, to take the Channel Ports and destroy the British Army. . . . There is no other course open to us but to fight it out. Every position must be held to the last man: there must be no retirement. With our backs

Manfred von Richthofen, fourth from left, chats to pilots from *Jasta* 10 a month before his death.

to the wall and believing in the justice of our cause each one of us must fight on to the end. The safety of our homes and the Freedom of mankind alike depend upon the conduct of each one of us at this critical moment.

While the British army dug in to defend their positions, the RAF went on the offensive. Throughout April 12 they bombed, strafed, and photographed the enemy, their contribution recognized subsequently by the *Official History*, which stated: "The advancing German divisions were subjected to relentless attacks by the British air squadrons. . . . [E]very squadron was used unsparingly from dawn to dusk."

The official historian neglected to mention the damage inflicted on the German air force. On April 12, forty-nine enemy aircraft were shot down, with a further twenty-five driven down "out of control." Nine days later von Richthofen was killed. The German air force had lost its greatest star, but not its fighting spirit, and by May 1918 the ranks of the RAF had thinned to an alarming degree.

Fresh blood was needed out in France, so the RAF turned to the cadets who had arrived in Oxford the previous fall. The understanding had always been that these young men would be trained by the British to fly in American squadrons, but, by May 1918, the American air force was not yet equipped to deploy to the front. So the U.S. Aviation Section of the Signal Corps agreed that its cadets could gain valuable experience by serving in the RAF until such a time as American squadrons began operations on the Western Front.

George Vaughn graduated from the School of Aerial Fighting at Ayr on May 2. The next day he traveled by train to London to take up an appointment that for many airmen was the last link in the chain before a posting to a combat squadron. "I am now what is called a 'Ferry Pilot'," he wrote to his family on May 3. "Which means I travel

Allied soldiers swarm over a downed German two-seater.

all around England flying machines from one airdrome to another, and then taking them over to France. When you get to France and deliver your machine you either fly another one back, or come back on boat. Then you repeat the process."

First Lieutenant Donald Poler was a month in advance of Vaughn, having started ferrying aircraft at the beginning of April. At the end of the month he "was assigned to the RAF pilots' pool in France . . . inland from Boulogne near Arras or St. Omer." Poler didn't remain long in the pilots' pool and in the first half of May he was posted to 40 Squadron. The squadron was one of the best in France, its renown built on the exploits of Mick Mannock and George McElroy. Neither ace was with the squadron when Poler arrived—Mannock had been appointed C.O. of 74 Squadron, and McElroy was recovering from a crash. Another of its luminaries, Maj. Leonard Tilney, had been shot down and killed in March.

Poler wasn't the only American posted to 40 Squadron to fill its depleted ranks. Mike Davis, a regular U.S. Army major, was there, as was Reed Landis. The British had learned from the mistakes of the previous two years when new pilots, untested in combat, were thrown into action almost immediately; having a new pilot come and go in the space of eleven days, as was the average life-expectancy twelve months earlier, served no purpose other than to demoralize the squadron. Now tyros were nurtured. "In the first two weeks at the No. 40 squadron we were conducted on what they called 'Cook's Tours,'" recalled Poler. "Up and down the front lines, getting used to the area, and being shown what to do and what not to do."[21]

First Lieutenant Bennett "Bim" Oliver was being handled in a similarly judicious manner. One of the fifty-two cadets who had sailed on the *Aurania* the previous summer, the Pittsburgh native was posted from the pilots' pool to 84 Squadron in May 1918, along with Alex Matthews, Morton Newhall, and Sam Eckert. Squadron commander was William Sholto Douglas, a man Oliver found "kept pretty much to himself." Nonetheless, Douglas had a high regard for the fighting qualities of American aviators having seen the damage inflicted on the enemy by Lt. Jens Frederick Larson. Inevitably

---

[21] Thomas Cook was a famous British travel agent of the nineteenth century whose company offered customers inclusive independent tours of all regions of the world.

nicknamed "Swede" in the squadron mess, the twenty-six-year-old Larson in fact hailed from Waltham, Massachusetts.

Like Fred Libby, Larson had worked his way into the war via Canada, enlisting in the 1st Canadian Overseas Contingent in February 1915, and serving in France as an artillery officer. It was a job that allowed him plenty of time to observe the air war, and the more Larson saw of it, the more he wanted to be part of this martial innovation. In October 1916 he successfully applied for a transfer to the RFC, and he was soon at Oxford, undergoing the same instruction that Oliver, Springs, and Grider would receive twelve months later.

Larson arrived at 84 Squadron in September 1917, and two months later shot down his first enemy aircraft. Bad weather in December curtailed his opportunities for further victims, but three days into the new year Larson claimed his second enemy aircraft. Two more followed in February, and on March 15 he achieved ace status when he downed a Pfalz D.III. A sixth victim fell to Larson's guns on March 18 and three days later, the same day that the Germans launched their massive ground offensive, the American departed for two weeks' leave in London.

William Sholto Douglas (right), C.O. of 84 Squadron, held his American pilots in high regard.

Introduced in January 1917, the D.III was an agile aircraft whose lower wing was reduced to allow greater downward visibility for the pilot—in this photo, the Red Baron himself.

Ten days into his furlough, a telegram arrived at his hotel ordering his return to France. Larson slipped back into the old routine almost at once, destroying two German aircraft on April 3 during a dogfight with "two formations of Pfalz and [Albatros D.III] V-strutters in the clouds at 7,000 ft." Larson, now a flight leader, led his four S.E.5s by example, diving through the clouds to ambush the enemy. "I got well on the tail of one at close range, firing with both guns," he wrote in his combat report. "The EA [enemy aircraft] turned under me; but I again got on his tail and fired both guns. The EA went down vertically, pulled out, stalled and started to spin." Larson then latched on to the tail of another V-strutter, "firing long bursts from both guns into him. The [EA] fell into a spin and I saw him crash into the ground about one mile east of Rosières."

On April 6, Larson claimed his ninth victim and then received orders to return to England to take up a post as an instructor. A little under a fortnight after Larson departed 84 Squadron, Oliver arrived at their base in Bertangles, a large airfield that they shared with Squadrons 23, 24, 48, 54, and 209.

When Oliver entered the mess on the evening of Sunday April 21, he found everyone "pretty well plastered. Someone thrust a glass into his hand and told him to join the party. Hadn't he heard? "We just buried Richthofen today."[22]

Oliver was mistaken in his belief that William Sholto Douglas was an aloof man; he was simply standing apart from the new recruits, observing them, scrutinizing their character, and—for his own curiosity as much as for the benefit of the squadron—discovering which Americans had volunteered to fight for the British from "a hot-headed zest for adventure" and which ones from "matters of stern principle." Not that it bothered him overly. Sholto Douglas found it "touching" that so many Americans had come to Britain's aid, and he reflected that "we of the Royal Air Force will always be grateful."

For several days Oliver and his fellow Americans practiced combat maneuvers over their own lines with their senior pilots. Then, when Douglas deemed them ready for combat, they went out on patrol. "On the first trip over the lines we crossed north of Amiens and very shortly met up with a flock of Albatros [and] a dogfight erupted," remembered Oliver.

Now was the time for Oliver to put into practice all that he'd been taught. For months he and his fellow American aviators had read the handbook distributed to them by the RFC entitled *On Aerial Combat* over and over again. In it were listed the four principles of air attack:

1. Open fire at the closest possible range.
2. Open fire under the most favorable conditions.
3. Open fire before the enemy does; if within reasonable range.
4. Give him no rest until you have downed him.

In addition, trainee aviators were advised to "reserve your fire until the last possible moment unless the enemy sees you and prepares to fire or actually fires." They should never engage the enemy with a half-finished drum of ammunition, and in attacking frontally, "always open fire at 200 yards because you will then be together before you

[22] Richthofen was actually buried a few days later, the RAF according him full military honors, with a four-bladed propeller in the shape of a cross as his headstone. His coffin was carried by six pilot officers of 3 Squadron, Australian Flying Corps, and the service was conducted by Rev. George Marshall. A month later, Oliver visited the grave and found it "pretty well desecrated . . . [T]he name plate and aluminum tips were gone and the cross had been chipped so that it looked like a skeleton." Richthofen's body was later exhumed and reburied in the family cemetery at Wiesbaden.

have fired your drum." Finally, if one should find an enemy aircraft on one's tail, "do not lose height if you can help it and do not do S turns." It was recommended that the pilot should perform an upward spiral, "at least until you have collected your thoughts."

Such advice was easy to absorb in the sanctuary of the classroom, but harder to apply when caught up in the first dogfight. Oliver later admitted he "didn't know at the time whether it was Piccadilly or Thursday night," so he disengaged and climbed above the fracas. "This may have been a bit on the saffron side but I'm still here and the C.O. [Douglas] seemed to think that I had done the right thing," he recalled.

Also at Bertangles aerodrome in May 1918 was 1st Lt. Frank Dixon, a graduate of the Princeton Flying School, who had come to England on board the *Carmania*. He was posted to 209 Squadron— Oliver LeBoutillier's squadron—arriving as a replacement for Captain Brown who had been "given leave for the Richthofen victory."

There was also a new squadron commander, Maj. John Andrews, the successor to Maj. Charles Butler, who had left 209 in the first week of May. Andrews was something of a legend within the RAF

Changing a 47-round drum from a Lewis gun was never easy for either pilot or observer.

by this stage of the war, a highly-decorated ace who had dueled with Max Immelmann and the Red Baron, and who had survived more than three years in the air. Andrews showed Dixon to his Sopwith Camel and told him to take up the aircraft and fire at some ground targets. Dixon recalled that Andrews was "a bit dissatisfied with my trials so he took the plane up and dived almost vertical before firing the guns."

Andrews climbed out of the Camel's cockpit and told Dixon with avuncular concern, "That's how I want you to do it. Don't level off so soon but watch the ground." However, Andrews couldn't always be there to nursemaid his charges; sometimes the novices had to learn on the job. "Another time I flew up to 18,000 ft with no oxygen," recalled Dixon, who said he began to descend when he felt giddy. "As I dived lower the plane suddenly hit dense air, snapped past the vertical and I found myself out of the seat belt and over the guns. . . . [T]he plane righted itself and I scrambled back to safety, though scared." It was another lesson learned by Dixon, who said the "rapid but thorough British training instilled confidence" in the new pilots.

While Dixon was still undergoing his initiation as a fighter pilot, another of the *Carmania* class had already claimed his first kill. Lloyd Hamilton, the son of a Methodist minister from Troy, and a former student at the Harvard Business School, had proved an outstanding pupil in England. Commissioned on March 2, 1918, Hamilton was posted to 3 Squadron under the command of Maj. Richard Raymond-Barker a fortnight later, at the same time as a South African pilot called Douglas Bell arrived from 27 Squadron. Bell had scored three victories with 27 Squadron, a feat in itself considering they had been equipped with the cumbersome Martinsyde biplanes, described by one RFC pilot, Cecil Lewis, as "so clumsy and un-manoeuvrable . . . they were sitting ducks."

Now let loose in a Sopwith Camel, Bell claimed twelve victories (including two observation balloons) in the space of a month, all the while bringing on Hamilton, until, on April 11, he took the American out on his first combat patrol. Hamilton swooped on an LVG between Courcelles and Ervillers but, despite firing 150 rounds, the German two-seater fled and the contact was marked "indecisive."

Such a glaring miss wasn't uncommon for new pilots. It took time to get one's eye in, for the brain and the trigger finger to harmonize; Hamilton required only a further twenty-four hours. On April 12, he shot down an Albatros, as did Bell, who then added a second

Major John Andrews, commander of 209 Squadron, was a leading British ace who had duelled with both Max Immelmann and the Red Baron and lived to tell the tale.

to round off a good day's hunting. Eight days later, Saturday April 20, Hamilton and 3 Squadron encountered a patrol of Richthofen's *Jagdstaffel* 11. The two squadron commanders engaged, the Red Baron against Major Raymond-Barker, and the German triumphed, sending the British ace crashing into the forest of Hamel in flames.

As Richthofen then turned his attention to the young Rhodesian pilot, Tommy Lewis, Hamilton picked out a blue Fokker triplane and opened fire. The German went into a spin and then flattened out, escaping the clutches of Hamilton who returned to a somber aerodrome. Their commanding officer was dead and Tommy Lewis a

Max Immelmann was an early German ace whose theories of combat flying were to influence the likes of the Red Baron .

prisoner, both victims of the Red Baron.

George Vaughn spent much of May in the hospital with influenza, one of the first victims of the pandemic that would kill tens of millions of people before the end of 1919. On May 23, the day after the Three Musketeers had arrived in France with 85 Squadron, Vaughn wrote his family from the American Expeditionary Headquarters: "I am out of hospital now, well and healthy again, and ready once more to go up to the front. The hospital provided a most comfortable place to be, with splendid quarters, food, and attention, but one cannot expect to spend the duration of the war in a hospital with the grippe."

Vaughn, who had celebrated his twenty-first birthday in the hospital, didn't have long to wait until he received his first posting. On May 25, he was assigned to 84 Squadron, another Yank to join Lts. Oliver, Matthews, Newhall, and Eckert. Vaughn was posted to B Flight under the command of a South African captain called Hugh Saunders. Straight away he knew he'd landed on his feet. "Sanders was a genial 230 pound veteran and was called 'dingbat'," recalled Vaughn. "He had a fine sense of humor and always found an amusing side to even dangerous situations."

Major Sholto Douglas also met with Vaughn's approval. Not at all the standoffish Englishman of Oliver's estimation, Sholto Douglas took an instant shine to his latest American, and together the pair formed the squadron band, the C.O. "playing on a set of traps made from old petrol tins while I played the piano in the officers' mess."

Vaughn was "indoctrinated into the ways of combat flying" under the careful tutelage of Saunders, but for the first ten days of his posting to 84 Squadron he was left on the ground whenever his fellow pilots went out on patrol. There were usually two patrols a day, one in the early morning, the other in the late afternoon. The strength of patrols varied. Sometimes two flights, with five aircraft per flight, went out; on other occasions Sholto Douglas ordered all three flights into the air.

The procedure was always the same, as Vaughn recalled: "After leaving Bertangles we would head straight west toward the Channel to gain altitude. When we finally could see the Channel, we would test our guns, and then turn toward the lines. We would cross the lines between 16,000 and 18,000 feet, with the leading flight usually from 1,000 to 2,000 feet lower than the second. The reason for this was that if the leading flight got into trouble, the second flight would come in with the superior altitude."

On June 2, Vaughn, still waiting for his first combat patrol, wrote home to tell his parents he had "been very fortunate in being posted to a good squadron where there are a very good bunch of fellows." Though he couldn't name names, he explained that "several of them I already knew when I arrived, having met them in England, so it

South African Hugh Saunders of 84 Squadron, known to George Vaughn as "dingbat."

made it very nice for me."

Two days later, Vaughn went on his first patrol, and on June 16, the squadron was ordered to provide an escort to a flight of bombers on a raid against German positions at Foucaucourt. On their return to Bertangles they were ambushed by two German fighters. One pilot quickly singled out Vaughn as a novice and "got a long burst into my tail before I knew he was even in the sky." Vaughn's luck was in. The German was no ace and his burst missed the target. Vaughn turned to his right and came out on the tail of his enemy. The German tried to shake off his pursuer but Vaughn clung to his quarry, following him for several miles east until eventually he poured a torrent of Vickers fire into the German. Smoke began billowing from the engine and "after falling some 500 feet it burst into flames."

Vaughn's first kill was confirmed by Alex Matthews and Roy Manzer, a Canadian from Victoria, but there was no jubilation when he landed at Bertangles. Waiting for him on the ground was Hugh Saunders, his giant frame quivering with rage. "Captain Saunders really read me off," remembered Vaughn. "He did not relish being pulled that far behind the lines just to watch over me."

Saunders had softened by the time dinner was served in the mess. A lesson had been learned, both by Vaughn and Saunders, who admired the pugnacity of his new officer. The next day Vaughn described his first kill in a letter to his family, an account that was sparse and lacking in glory. "It was not a large fight by any means," he said, "but large enough for a starter, as it is the first fight I have been in." Vaughn's excuse for not writing more was that it was tea-time and "even out here in France the English stick to their afternoon tea."

"Honestly," he added, "I am so used to it now that I don't know how I will do without it when I go to the American army. The Americans, by the way are doing some fine work over here, and get some very good 'write ups' in the papers."

CHAPTER 9

Am I to Blame?

May 1918 found Arthur Taber still at the 3rd Air Instructional Center in Issoudun, as far away from becoming a fighter pilot as ever. Instead, as he explained in a letter to his parents, he was the center's officer of the guard, "keeping records and doing paper work all day, and inspecting every guard on his post in the camp three times a night." Ever the dutiful son, however, Taber made sure he wrote to his mother on May 12 to wish her a happy Mother's Day, and to assure her he was being as virtuous as ever. In fact, only that morning he had been at Sunday service where the sermon centered on "the responsibility of the men in the A.E.F. to live straight so that they may go home untainted and fit to cope with the problems of America as the greatest world-power."

Nearly a fortnight later, Saturday May 25, the ladies of the Red Cross canteen gave a dance for the Center's officers to which "several truck-loads of nurses were imported from a hospital near here." Taber rated the nurses "not too impressive," but fortunately the refined ladies of the Red Cross were more to his delectation and he "found several good dancers." It was, he told his sister, an enjoyable evening and he hoped "more of such hops will be held for a diversion."

On the same Saturday night that Arthur Taber was dancing with the ladies of the Red Cross canteen, the Three Musketeers were still settling into their new home at Petite Synthe, just a couple of miles from the French coastal city of Dunkirk. Elliott Springs wrote his father that he "was at peace with the world." The move to France had intensified the camaraderie within 85 Squadron and Springs

Some of 85 Squadron. From left to right: Springs, Horn, Langton, Callahan, Dymmand, Thompson, and Brown.

was writing the letter moments after Billy Bishop had provided some entertainment by inadvertently using cold cream for toothpaste. Boy, how they'd laughed—all except Bishop's orderly.

The airfield at Petite Synthe was in a rough triangle "between the main railway line from Dunkirk to Calais, the by-road running from Petite Synthe to Pont de Petite Synthe on the Bourbourg Canal, and the sidings of the railway on which hospital trains belonging to the French Medical Corps were drawn up." Springs's equable state of mind may also have owed something to the surroundings: the aerodrome was appealingly bucolic, a delightful patchwork of colors—varying shades of greens, browns, and grays—with the road to the squadron's home lined by a row of tall, elegant poplars.

There were no dances or parties for 85 Squadron that night, nor would there be for the foreseeable future, but Springs wasn't bereft. On the contrary, as he told his father, "it's a great relief to be sure that it will be at least six months before you're going to see a woman again, that is anything eligible. . . . [Y]ou should see the difference in the squadron in France and in England. In England the chief consideration is feminine as in the States and the fellowship is somewhat neglected. Over here the detraction and distraction is removed and you can see what a man's world is really like. And strange to say, our social graces improve. We don't lapse into a state of degenerate coma as is the popular supposition. Woman's refining influence is not missed at all."

The next day, Sunday May 26, Springs and the other untested pilots of 85 Squadron began familiarizing themselves with their sector, under the eye of Captain Horn. The squadron was scheduled to become operational on June 1, but Bishop couldn't wait that long. Out of combat since April 1917, he went out looking for the enemy and he soon found one. "The major bags a Hun!" wrote a starstruck Springs in his diary on May 26. "Major Bishop is unquestionably the greatest fighter of the age."

John McGavock Grider thought so, too, exhorting his sister in a letter to buy Bishop's book. "It will you give you some idea of the man I am with," he declared. "He is one of the best and we all love him."

On May 27, Bishop added two more victims to his score, the major setting an example that the squadron's other aces felt obliged to match. Captain Benbow went out in hunt of a "nice fat Hun," but encountered six and was chased back to base under fire. "He was awfully fed up about it," wrote Springs, who found it comical that the Englishman always flew wearing a monocle rather than goggles. Benbow swore vengeance and the next day took off to find his ninth victim of the war. Instead, he found another ace, Hans-Eberhardt Gandert of *Jasta* 51, who shot down and killed the monocle-wearing Benbow.

The following day was another mixed one for the squadron. Bishop bagged his customary German but Captain B. A. Baker and a pilot called Brown both crashed, although neither was seriously injured.

Springs and Grider went into Dunkirk to stock up on essentials, the most important of which was toothpaste. Neither knew the French word so Springs made his desires known to the young blonde sales assistant while Grider gave a running commentary on her appearance. "You've got a pretty face but a square ankle," was one of his judgments, much to the amusement of Springs, who nudged his friend in the ribs and told him to quit making him laugh.

When the time came to pay the sales assistant glared at the pair and asked in flawless English: "Do you want it wrapped or will you take it in your pocket?" The two Americans fled in embarrassment.

A graver miscalculation ensued on the last day of May, when Springs spotted a German patrol 200 feet beneath him, over Armentières. Alone but full of confidence, Springs saw that one of the six enemy aircraft was straggling behind the others. This was irresistible! If Bishop could kill at will, then so could Springs. He dived on the German and opened fire, missing the target, and alerting the rest of the patrol to his audacity. In a matter of seconds Springs was again fleeing, only this time it was to escape a "peppering" from six German fighters. "I hadn't the faintest idea what to do," he admitted the next day in a letter to his stepmother. "I knew what the major would do—turn and shoot a couple of them down and chase the rest of them home—but somehow or other I thought I needed a little more experience before trying that."

Springs dived—"wondering mildly how long before my wings would fall off"—and eventually the Germans gave up the chase, and retreated back to the safety of their own lines. Back at Petite Synthe Springs was "the joke of the squadron," with Grider "in hysterics" at his friend's foolhardiness.

Bishop was less amused. Springs had fallen for the same trick that Benbow had a few days earlier, attacking a "straggler" when in fact he was the bait laid by the Germans. For the next few days, Bishop told Springs, he would "tag along" with him so he could better keep an eye on the impetuous American.

The next day Springs, now considered the secretary of the "Sadder-but-Wiser" club, went on patrol with Bishop, Horn, and Capt. Malcolm McGregor, a New Zealander with two kills to his credit. It wasn't long before they spotted the German patrol, with what Springs called "my six friends" laying the same trap for their enemy. This time, however, the hunters became the hunted, and only two of the Germans escaped with their lives. Of the other four, two were shot down by McGregor, one by Bishop, and one by Springs.[23]

However, Springs was still not satisfied. He set off after the two Germans fleeing east, but quickly "decided that discretion was the better part of valor." His decision was influenced by a ferocious blizzard of anti-aircraft (A.A.) fire as he flew deeper into German territory. "About three Hun Archie batteries opened on me and the

[23] In his correspondence, Springs misspelled the name as "MacGregor."

whole sky turned black," he wrote to his stepmother. "Pooof, pooof, right under my wing tips goes Archie and my heart beats 200 higher. Pooof, pooof, he's got my range again, dive quick, then turn and climb. This won't do, I'll run for it."

As Springs knew from the veteran pilots, it wasn't the A.A. bursts one heard that were dangerous, rather those one didn't that did the damage. But Springs was lucky. The German gunners couldn't get his range and he returned to base intact.[24]

Bishop's remarkable success rate continued into June, the major downing six enemy aircraft over a three-day period to reclaim his mantle of leading ace from the British pilot, James McCudden. Springs failed to add to his tally, but nonetheless the fact he had one made him a "changed man." He had shot down a German, thus proving himself a combat pilot in the eyes of the squadron, and that gave him "sensations I never knew existed before."

Larry Callahan experienced a similar excitement when, on June 4, he, Bishop, and a Canadian pilot called Herbert Thomson, took on a German patrol. Bishop and Thomson shot down one each, and Callahan sent a long burst into his adversary. Callahan's aircraft wasn't seen to crash so he returned to base unable to say he had emulated Springs.[25]

The procedure for claiming a victory was complex for Allied pilots, as most engagements were fought over German lines, rendering emphatic confirmation virtually impossible. Upon returning from a patrol a pilot would complete a combat report in which a number was entered for one of three categories: 1) Destroyed. 2) Driven down out of control. 3) Driven down.

Once approved by the commanding officer, the form would be sent to Wing Headquarters, then Brigade headquarters, and finally on to RAF Command in France, where staff officers "had the advantage of cross checks not available at lower levels." Using the limited intelligence at their disposal—information from observation posts and other squadron's combat reports—they would then rate the pilot's claim "Decisive" or "Indecisive."

[24] British A.A. fire produced white bursts. In the handbook issued to new pilots, *On Aerial Combat*, students were left in no doubt as to the threat posed by German ground fire. "The Germans put up barrages at different levels and often wait to catch our machines when they are maneuvering prior to attacking enemy formations."

[25] Some sources spell Thomson's surname with a *p*.

Although neither Callahan nor Grider had yet to emulate Springs's feat of downing a German, both were adjusting to the physical demands of daily patrolling. It was early summer in France but at 18,000 feet it was still cold as hell and liable to make a pilot sleepy. (Two thousand feet higher, the average temperature was minus ten degrees.) Springs complained of such a condition in a letter home dated June 6, also informing his father that "my ears are very sore from high altitudes and long dives and my eyes are rather sore from flying without goggles." He added that no one wore goggles when "you're out hunting," since painful eyes were a small price to pay for an unobstructed view. Being exposed to the elements in the small

Exposed to the elements at 20,000 feet, pilots often had to improvise, as this one is doing wearing a leather mask to protect his face.

cockpit of the S.E.5a resulted in other afflictions: split lips, frostbite, and headaches. Pilots were taught to "swallow or hold your nostrils and blow to relieve the pressure on your ears" when descending; fine in training but not so practical when diving to escape an enemy patrol.

A device called a "peter tube" allowed pilots to urinate, but that was a challenge in itself when most took to the air wearing three pairs of gloves (silk as a base layer, then chamois, and then "a heavy pair of flying gloves over the lot").

Springs, however, was blessed with an iron constitution, and could cope with the physical demands of flying. It was day-to-day living that was proving problematic in early June. "I'm having great difficulty getting liquor," he complained to his diary. Eventually the Three Musketeers could stand it no more and, on June 6, they went to Boulogne on a booze run. "Bring back a lot," wrote Springs. "Inside us."

On June 11, the squadron moved twenty miles south to a new aerodrome at St. Omer. The airstrip wasn't up to much, but everyone was impressed with their quarters; instead of the tents of Petite Synthe, the pilots were quartered in Nissen huts, and Grider considered the Mess "wonderful." He added in a letter home: "We have a piano which Larry [Callahan] tries to paw to pieces every night, a phonograph and hundreds of the latest records, the best food in France, and one of our A.M.s [air mechanics] is an artist. He is decorating the mess hall and the ante-rooms. We are comfortable and happy."

Grider had been blooded in combat on June 9 when he clashed with a German fighter during a dogfight. The pair had turned and half-rolled, trying to maneuver into a firing position, before the German broke off the attack and headed east "with Mac still popping at him."

Callahan rated Grider "an excellent shot," and a man of "very great determination [who] was willing to take any kind of chance there was." He had only one weakness, in Callahan's eyes: Grider "was a fairly ham-handed pilot."

Grider told his sister she needn't "worry about anything happening to me," as he was in the best squadron in France; he reiterated his desire to return to Arkansas and see out his days on the San Souci plantation.

Three weeks after arriving in France, the bravado of the Three Musketeers had lost some of its luster. They now appreciated there was no dishonor in running from a fight if there were four of

85 Squadron poses for a photograph in France, believed to be taken in June or July 1918.

them and one of you; only a fool—or an idiot—would take on such odds. They had learned, too, how to watch the sun for direction when spinning or turning, so as not to become disorientated and crash into the earth, and A.A. fire they treated with respect, but not terror.

June 17, 1918, was a highly important day for the Three Musketeers. In the previous nine months they had got drunk together, chased women together, trained together, laughed and cried together, and now they were going on patrol together.

Their three S.E.5s took off from St. Omer early in the morning and crossed into what they called "Hunland" at 15,000 feet. Springs saw a flash of light "five miles ahead of me and 2,000 feet below." He waggled his wings, pointed toward the light, and led his two friends toward the target. In the German two-seater, the observer had seen the threat and was behind his machine-gun waiting for the three aircraft to come into range. What he failed to note, however, was the approach of Lt. John Canning, another 85 Squadron pilot, who had spotted the enemy aircraft at the same time as the Three Musketeers. "They dived from behind and I dived in from in front and slightly to one side," he wrote in his combat report. "Opened fire at 100 yards and emptied one drum of Lewis and 100 rounds from my Vickers into the center section and engine of the E.A., which burst into flames."

As Canning broke off his attack he identified Grider "right on the E.A.'s tail, his tracers seemed to be going into the observer's cockpit." The American's own report on the incident concluded with his glancing over his shoulder as "the E.A. crashed in a cloud of flame and smoke."

Back in the mess, the Three Musketeers whooped and hollered, "feeling very proud of ourselves." Springs told everyone that he'd been so close to the burning Hun he felt the heat from the flames. Grider said he'd kept on firing till he was no more than twenty-five yards from the enemy aircraft.

The next morning, June 18, the Three Musketeers took an early breakfast of coffee, shredded wheat, and eggs benedict. The men felt no apprehension. The war was still fun. It was agreed Grider would lead this time and flush out any lonesome Germans. Out on the airfield, however, bad news awaited Callahan. His engine wasn't firing properly, and his mechanics said they needed time to resolve the problem. Grider, meanwhile, was dismayed to discover that his lucky mascot, the doll given him by Billie Carleton, was not in his aircraft. It had been damaged the previous day, and one of the ground crew had promised to have it repaired and returned by the morning.

Callahan watched as his two friends took off into an overcast sky and headed due east toward the town of Menin in Belgium. The pair climbed to 16,000 feet and flew deep into enemy territory, their eyes scanning the sky to the front and the rear. Suddenly they saw a German two-seater several thousand feet below them and a couple of miles to the east.

This time Springs dove onto the enemy's tail firing "one Lewis drum and Vickers from immediately behind." The German observer, gamely standing in his cockpit blazing away with his machine gun, was trapped in a deluge of fire. Springs could see tracer rounds shredding his body. He broke away in a climbing turn, and together with Grider watched as the Rumpler reconnaissance plane toppled from the sky with neither noise nor flame.

Callahan was still on the aerodrome when Springs returned. As his friend taxied along the grass runway, the ground crew running excitedly over to hear if he had had a good morning's hunting, Callahan continued to scan the sky. "Where's Mac?" he asked. Springs didn't know; he couldn't understand where his friend had got to. However, he wasn't worried, sure that Grider would soon appear, and entertain them all with some hilarious escapade.

At lunch there was still no sign of Grider, nor was there when 85 Squadron took their seats in the mess for dinner. Springs returned to his billet, sat on his bed and opened his diary. "Mac missing," he wrote. "Oh Christ. Am I to blame."

CHAPTER 10

From Toronto to the Trocadero

On the morning of May 27, 1918, four days after the Three Musketeers had arrived in France with 85 Squadron, the third battle of the Aisne began. Four thousand German artillery guns erupted along a twenty-four-mile stretch of the Allied lines as the Kaiser's army attacked positions on the Chemin des Dames ridge, in the Aisne River region of France, approximately eighty miles northeast of Paris.

The attack was a stunning success, German soldiers advancing behind a cloud of poison gas to reach the Aisne in just six hours. By nightfall on May 27, the German army had pushed more than twenty-five miles into Allied territory, demoralizing eight enemy divisions and seizing an estimated fifty thousand prisoners. By June 3, German troops were within thirty-five miles of Paris, and panic began to grip the city's inhabitants.

However, Gen. Erich Ludendorff had asked too much of his men in too short a period. The German supply line began to creak, casualties mounted, exhaustion increased, and then the American 3rd Division arrived to take up positions on the south bank of the Marne near Château-Thierry. They were green troops, but they were fresh and eager to prove themselves to their British and French Allies.

So, too, were the two American pilots flying S.E.5s in 32 Squadron. Lieutenants Bogart Rogers and Alvin Callender were both untested in aerial warfare, but as anxious as the infantry to show

Bogart Rogers, a twenty-year-old Californian, arrived at 32 squadron in the early summer of 1918 with a devil-may-care attitude.

what they could do. On Sunday June 2, the squadron commander, Maj. John Russell, was ordered to move seventy miles south to Fouquerolles, near the town of Beauvais. The role of 32 Squadron was twofold: to escort observation planes; and strafe enemy soldiers, artillery, and transport.

Rogers, a twenty-year-old Californian, wrote his girlfriend, Isabelle Young, "a petite history major with a lovely soprano voice," whom he had wooed while they were students at Stanford University. "We have been ordered to be ready to move and have been packed for two days. Like Mohammet, if the war won't come to us, we shall go to the war. Apparently that's what is going to happen. If we move where we expect to we'll get a lot of hard work."

Rogers finished the letter, snuffed out his candle, and settled down to sleep. Minutes later he heard heavy steps on the stairs and the door to his billet was flung open. It was Major Russell. "Rogers, everything to be packed in half an hour," barked the Englishman. "Only keep out what things you can carry in a haversack in your machine."

Rogers did as instructed, loading his belongings with the help of his orderly on to one of several trucks. Around three in the morning the convoy departed for Fouquerolles. Russell told his pilots to get their heads down for a couple of hours. They would fly south in the morning. Rogers and his friend Alvin Callender "went up to the aerodrome, crawled into flying suits and climbed up on top of the hangars for a few hours' sleep." For Callender it must have been a strange moment, sleeping under the stars in northern France, almost twelve months to the day after enlisting in the RFC.

Alvin Callender wrote his mother in May 1918 that he didn't "think much" of the war.

Alvin Andrew Callender was born on July 4, 1893, in New Orleans. He studied architecture at Tulane University before youthful restlessness got the better of him. Designing buildings could wait; adventure couldn't. He joined the Louisiana National Guard's Washington Artillery and served on the Mexican border in 1916 during the Pancho Villa hostilities. That disturbance only temporarily slaked Callender's thirst for excitement; he craved more, and he figured enlisting in the RFC would be the quickest way to get into "a bit of a scrap." Callender looked like a man who enjoyed a scrap: he had a strong jaw, broad shoulders, and a hard, intense look in his eyes.

He joined the RFC in the first week of June 1917, and trod the well-worn path from the Cadet Wing of the University of Toronto to Deseronto, "a little country town on the north bank of the

St. Lawrence about half way between Toronto and Montreal." After graduating from training, Callender was shipped out to England, and a month later, April 1918, he was posted to 32 Squadron, joining them at Beauvois (not to be confused with the town of Beauvais to the south).

Bogart Rogers's posting to the squadron was even more precipitous. On April 23, he was writing to his fiancée from the School of Aerial Fighting in Ayr, telling her how he was playing a lot of golf to while away the hours. Five days later he was in France.

So far Rogers liked what he saw of 32 Squadron. The mess wasn't much to write home about, "a dingy little building on a corner with 'Au Trocadero' in large red letters over the door," but the men inside were first-rate. "The O.C. [Maj. John Russell] is very popular [and] the fellows seem to be far above the ordinary," he told his fiancée. One of the fellows was an Irish ace from Belfast by the name of Walter Tyrell. He was little more than a boy, being only nineteen, but, when Rogers arrived in the mess, he was pointed out as the squadron's top ace with ten kills. The next day Tyrell took his tally to thirteen, and Rogers, even though a year his senior, wrote home of the event with juvenile infatuation.

Rogers and Callender settled smoothly into the squadron routine, one which Rogers depicted to his fiancée in a letter home. Having first described how the squadron was on standby from 0930, Rogers wrote that often it was not until the late afternoon that they were called upon to escort a bomber squadron on a raid over enemy lines. In such a case: Major Russell briefs the pilots on the mission, ordering them to be ready to take off at 1600 hours. Half an hour before that appointed time, the ground crew wheel out the aircraft from the hangars and at 1545 hours the engines are started. The pilots emerge from the mess, where they've just taken tea, and walk across the grass to their machines dressed in their flying kit, talking, joking, and maintaining an air of insouciance. A last word with the squadron commander, a final check of the map, and then the pilots climb into the cockpits. He straps himself in, arranges everything to his satisfaction, checks the mascot is in place, and then runs up his motor, slowly at first, then to maximum power as a mechanic clings to each wing and a third holds on to the tail of the S.E.5.

Once the pilot is happy, his hand goes up and the blocks come out from under the wheels. The aircraft begins to taxi out to take

Walter Tyrell of 32 Squadron was a dashing Irish ace whose luck ran out in June 1918.

off, waiting for the flight commander to lead them up. The rest follow in their given formation and, after a couple of turns of the airfield, the flight heads off into the sky.[26]

On May 16, Rogers was a member of an offensive patrol that flew south-east into the German lines. As he explained later to his fiancée, his eyes had yet to acquire the sharpness of their experienced pilots. At 14,000 feet, his flight commander, Capt. Sturley Simpson—a former British infantry officer who never took to the air without a lavender silk handkerchief in his pocket—turned due east and dived. For a moment or two Rogers was nonplussed. Then he saw six enemy fighters on the tail of a British R.E.8 reconnaissance plane. Glancing above him Rogers spotted six more Germans, "nasty looking machines with big black crosses and painted in gaudy colors." Rogers's flight was the meat in a Flying Circus sandwich, but fortunately for the British another flight from 32 Squadron was close on hand to spoil the enemy feast.

[26] John H. Morrow and Earl Rogers, eds., *A Yankee Ace in the RAF*

"The first thing that came to my mind was having been told that when a Hun was on one of your machines' tails, open fire no matter what the range," he wrote to his fiancée. "You probably won't shoot him down but he'll quickly lose interest in his target when a few bullets whizz by. So down I went motor full on, got a squirt at one little purple and white devil, and let him have both guns. In the meantime Hun tracers streaked by leaving thin smoke trails and darn near scaring me to death. I pulled out, did a climbing turn, half rolled and dived again. Just as a grand dog fight was about to start, one of the guns jammed and I pulled away. It was all over in less than a minute, for all of the Huns dived east and disappeared."

Later on in the mess Rogers joined in the retelling of the scrap. The veterans slapped him on the back, thrust a beer into his hands, and assured him the first dogfight was always the worst. What mattered most wasn't shooting down a Hun, but returning alive. Back in his quarters, Rogers confessed to his fiancée: "Everything happens so quickly in a scrap that one hasn't time to think, scarcely time to act. I surely was scared blue."

The British R.E.8 reconnaissance plane was easy meat for the German fighters.

Ground crew hold on to the ailerons. These unsung heroes were vital in each squadron.

Alvin Callender missed the dogfight on May 16. The previous day a cylinder on his engine cracked during an offensive patrol and he lost all his water through the exhaust, forcing him to crash land near Crepy. Callender spent a frustrating day badgering his mechanics to hurry up and install his new engine.

Ground crews were the unsung heroes of every squadron, described by Air Marshal Hugh Trenchard as "the backbone of our effort." Nonetheless at every aerodrome in France there was a "them and us" attitude between the pilots and the ground crew. Pilots were officers, the ground crew were not; the social distinction was like a chill breeze sweeping the aerodrome. No fitter or rigger or armorer could ever enter the pilots' mess and dine at the same table as a lieutenant or captain.

Nonetheless most pilots respected and relied upon their ground crew, who, in some squadrons numbered two hundred. "They carry a great responsibility," wrote Fred Libby. "One little slip or mistake by your ground crew would be curtains for a ship, the pilot and observer."

With the responsibility came pride. Ground crews were proud of their work, and prouder still of their pilots. Every enemy aircraft shot down was one for their own tally, just as a gun jam or a cracked cylinder was a source of anxiety. But nothing was worse than the death of a favorite pilot. "I have seen them standing out on the edge of our landing field, scanning the skies, hoping against hope that by some chance they will see their ship returning long after the time has passed when their pilot should be home," Libby wrote.

Callender had to sit on the edge of the conversation on the night of May 16, listening to an account of the dogfight, hearing of the sharpshooting of Lt. Wilfred Green, who had shot down a Pfalz; the Albatros blasted at point-blank range by wee Jerry Flynn, a nineteen-year-old Canadian "devil," and the smallest man in the squadron. The grandest man in the squadron was Capt. Edmond William Claude Gerard de Vere Pery, also known as Lord Glentworth, son of the Earl of Limerick. However, no one used his title in the mess: he was just one of the boys, and "a fine chap" to Bogart, who shared a room with his lordship. He was a fine shot, too, and had accounted for two Germans in the dogfight.

Two days later the Viscount went off on an early morning sortie with 1st Lt. Parr Hooper, a twenty-five-year-old from Baltimore recently arrived at the squadron. They attacked a pair of German two-seater aircraft over Etaing, but heavy and accurate fire from the observers drove them off. Hooper saw the Viscount's aircraft go into a spin. There was no smoke, no flames, and the aircraft didn't appear to be damaged. Hooper watched as the Viscount wrestled with his machine, struggling to bring it under control as the German ground fire intensified. Back at base the American made out his report. It was garbled and indefinite, Hooper unable to say with any certainty if the Viscount was alive, but he thought he'd seen him jump clear of the aircraft.

"Being a gentleman of some importance close enquiries were made," Rogers wrote his fiancée a few days later. The news came back that the Viscount was dead.

Callender's frustration grew as May deepened without his seeing any action. "After looking over this here war, I don't think much of it," he wrote to his mother on May 27. Despite one or two patrols a day, always well into German territory, he'd only caught sight of enemy aircraft away in the distance. They had no inclination for a scrap, "so barring unavoidable accidents, such as might happen in a street car at home, I'll be back for a Christmas dinner in about six months."

Callender's luck changed the following day. This time the Germans his flight encountered "did not turn east and beat it," but instead came to fight. There were four beneath Callender's patrol and nine above. Another 32 Squadron patrol, led by Captain Simpson, engaged the Germans above, leaving Callender and his flight commander, Capt. Arthur Claydon, a Canadian from Winnipeg, to deal with the four Pfalz. Two escaped but two were caught, Claydon downing one, Callender the other. "I got about 75 shots into him before he turned over and fell out of control," he wrote his mother a couple of days later. " . . . so this Hun is up playing with the angels now anyway instead of dropping bombs on hospitals."

CHAPTER 11

Chills Down My Spine

On June 3, 1918, 32 Squadron moved seventy miles south from Beauvois to Fouquerolles, one of nine RAF squadrons (162 aircraft in total) detailed to augment the stretched French air service struggling to cope with the latest German offensive.

Their new aerodrome was deserted when Rogers and his fellow pilots touched down. The column of trucks containing the ground crews and equipment had yet to arrive. With nothing to do Major Russell led his men into Fouquerolles. They found a small café where the owner was delighted to see airmen. Airmen meant money and soon she was serving them all "horrible wine and lemonade."[27]

The move south had brought 32 Squadron closer to the war. Two nights after their arrival, there was an air raid on Fouquerolles, and, on June 5, the squadron had what Rogers described to his fiancée as a "stiff scrap" with several German Albatross. Callender had a lucky escape, said Rogers, his S.E.5 going down "for several thousand feet belching flames and smoke. . . . [I]t surely looked like curtains for him but he dove the fires out and came home with nothing worse than a pale face and rather shaky nerves."

Callender made light of the terrifying incident in his own account, written to his sister on June 8. He began the letter in characteristically chest-thumping fashion. "It's a lovely war," he declared,

---

[27] John H. Morrow and Earl Rogers, eds., *A Yankee Ace in the RAF*

Aircraft, such as this Camel, could receive terrible superficial damage in combat and still return safely to base.

before giving a flourishing account of his second victory. Set upon by an Albatros, Callender evaded the enemy fire and then turned on his assailant, already running for home. "He certainly was funny," he recounted. "I laughed so hard I could hardly shoot because he was such a fool, he shot wild, turned and dived. I whipped my machine over as soon as I heard him, and was right on top of him with both guns going."

As for his own brush with death, Callender had little to say. A bullet had set ablaze his fuel tank, but "when the petrol was all burnt out it went out without spreading, and I had enough gas in my tank to finish the patrol."

Rogers was assigned a new roommate following the death of Viscount Glentworth, a recent arrival by the name of Lt. Eric Jarvis. He was pleasant, unassuming, quiet but courteous, and at once Rogers feared for him. "Honestly, Izzy," he wrote his fiancée.

"When I wake up in the morning and look over at him, I can hardly keep from weeping. A more melancholy looking person can't exist."

Some pilots seemed marked for death the moment they arrived at a squadron, as if stalked by the grim reaper. More often than not they were docile men, ones who lacked the necessary aggression, even the nastiness, to survive a "scrap" or a "show" with the enemy. Others kept ahead of their nemesis for weeks, months, until finally its shadow fell upon them. Fred Libby remembered how life began draining from one of his friends in 43 Squadron. "For some reason he doesn't seem up to par," wrote Libby. "He seems to have something on his mind." The pilot began to question his own ability, began asking Libby "what he has been doing wrong in his last flights." Libby tried to reassure him that he had done nothing wrong, but to no avail. A few days later he was killed in a dogfight.

Premonitions were not uncommon among pilots. Lt. John Southey, an experienced member of 24 Squadron, recalled one June afternoon in 1918 when a mild-mannered pilot called James Dawe foresaw his own death as he sat in a deck chair. Southey and a couple of other pilots were playing a popular RAF game called bumble-puppy [the equivalent of swingball or tetherball]. "I asked him to have a game," recalled Southey. "He refused and just sat brooding in his chair and was very quiet. He appeared to be under stress and seemed to bite his tongue as he sat there." Dawe failed to return from a patrol the next day.

The men who coped best with the specter of death were those who accepted the odds. Nearly every pilot would crash at some stage, surmised Elliott Springs in March 1918, either by accident or as a result of enemy fire. "It's absolutely unavoidable," he wrote his step-mother. "Every time a man goes up he's flirting with the undertaker and every time he makes a landing he's kidding the three Fates about their scythes being dull."

Celebrate life and don't think about death, was Springs's motto. If it happens, it happens. So, too, Rogers, who went to France a fatal-ist. "It was the only doctrine that would hold water," he wrote. "If you embraced it, as many did, it was a great source of consolation. You simply decided your destiny was predetermined and inevi-table and ceased worrying about what might happen to you. When your time came it would come, there was nothing you could do to stop it."

Pilots, like these ones from 40 Squadron, tried to relax during missions, but by the summer of 1918 the stress of combat was drawing a heavy toll.

Lieutenant Eric Jarvis was returning from a patrol with 32 Squadron on June 6 when he stalled his aircraft on the approach to the airfield. The machine crashed to the ground from 200 feet and Jarvis died the same day in hospital. The death of such a callow pilot didn't weigh heavily on the shoulders of the rest of the squadron. There was almost an element of natural selection in a frontline squadron. But three days after the death of Jarvis came the shattering news of Walter Tyrell's demise, shot down by ground fire as the squadron strafed enemy positions near Audechy. Rogers was just one of several pilots who saw Tyrell's aircraft smash into the ground from 1,000 feet. The next day, June 10, brought another death, this time Parr Hooper who spiraled into the ground after being hit during a bombing mission. "The short time that he was in the squadron he proved himself to be exceedingly brave and a good leader," Major Russell wrote to Hooper's father. "He will be a great loss to the Flying Corps, the U. S. Flying Corps, and especially to this squadron at the present time."

Fear began to grip even the squadron's most experienced pilots. They were no longer patrolling the sky searching for dogfights; they were strafing and bombing enemy transport, troops, and gun emplacements. It was hateful work. "Going fifteen miles over the lines at 2,000 feet, getting machine-gunned from the ground and archied all over the place is not my idea of a peaceful Sunday," Rogers informed his fiancée. He described how he'd dropped four bombs on a road crowded with enemy troops, then swooped down to machine gun whatever he saw. "We were practically flying thru a barrage of shells, the Hun tracers streaking by uncomfortably close," he continued. "It can't be described. Finally after many darn good attempts archie got me and nearly ripped one aileron away, a great ragged hole that almost cut the controls and shattered the aileron."

The explosives dropped by 32 Squadron were 20-pound Cooper bombs (which weighed 25 pounds when the explosive charge and fuse were fitted), carried on a rack under one of the S.E.5s' wings.

British fighters carried 25-pound Cooper bombs for low-level bombing missions.

Each aircraft had four bombs in total and pilots released them in pairs, starting with the two on the outside. Upon release the "nose spinner was freed to turn which then rotated a plate in the nose, which eventually exposed the detonator to a firing mechanism, which would be activated when the bomb struck a solid object."

On June 9, Callender's six-strong flight bombed an anti-aircraft battery east of Roye, but only two aircraft returned to base. No one was killed, but it was indication of the perils facing the squadron. Callender had been forced down by a broken propeller, a problem that was soon repaired so he was able to participate in an afternoon offensive patrol. In the evening the American was in the air again, on a bombing mission led by Major Russell himself. Callender dropped bombs on an A.A. battery near Faverolles and avoided the ferocious ground fire directed his way.

There was no rest for Callender. The next day, he and Claydon bombed another gun battery, only this time a flight of enemy aircraft was lying in wait among the clouds. Four Fokker D.VIIs went after Claydon; the other four targeted the American. Then nine more came into view.

The Fokker had entered service two months earlier, the most recent addition to the German air force and rated by Manfred von Richthofen as a brilliant fighting machine. He'd tested the prototype in January 1918 "and was so enthusiastic that he delayed reequipping his J.G.1." A biplane of cantilever wing design with no external bracing, the Fokker D.VII was powered with a 185-horsepower BMW engine, could hit 130 miles per hour in level flight, and was capable of climbing to 13,200 feet in ten minutes.

The S.E.5s turned tail and fled for their lines, chased all the way by the Fokkers. Callender later counted eight bullet holes in his fuselage and one in his engine. "I hope my luck keeps with me," he wrote to his mother two days later.

The low-level flying eased slightly in the days that followed. There was time to sit in the sunshine, gorging on strawberries and cherries. Some pilots challenged each other to games of tennis on an improvised court, others went into town and got drunk on cheap wine. Rogers and Callahan wrote letters home, reveling in their sudden "sweet slumber." Callender told his mother he found the war "an interesting diversion with its enjoyable points."

On June 28, the squadron moved north again, this time to an aerodrome at Ruisseauville, approximately twenty miles south-west

The Fokker D.VII had a 185-horsepower BMW engine, could hit 130 miles per hour in level flight, and was capable of climbing to 13,200 feet in ten minutes.

of 85 Squadron at St. Omer, which they shared with a squadron of bombers. If the rumors were true, the Germans were about to launch a big offensive in Flanders.

However, there was no offensive, at least not in the first week of July. Callender found time to read an English translation of von Richthofen's memoirs, *The Red Battle Flyer*, and Springs wrote a long letter home about the number of popcorn vendors in Los Angeles: thirty-two, of whom twenty-nine were Italian. On July 4, the squadron threw an Independence Day party for its two Americans, a lavish affair with the mess decorated in red, white, and blue and draped with a Stars and Stripes. The menu consisted of crab salad, soup, fish, chicken, cauliflower, asparagus, strawberries, nuts, and coffees, "to say nothing of liquid refreshment."

The airmen were still partying at two in the morning and one or two of the abstemious pilots wondered what would happen if orders came through for a dawn mission. But dawn on July 5 rolled back to

The von Richthofen brothers, Manfred and Lothar, are in the center of this group of Circus pilots.

reveal thick cloud. God was clearly an American, said Rogers, who, like everyone else, slept until noon.

Three days later, July 8, Callender shot down his third German, a Fokker D.VII, though another "sent streams of lead past my ear and chills down my spine." Rogers was still searching for his first victim but instead found himself detailed to chaperon several new pilots on an afternoon patrol. He found it an irksome assignment, mollycoddling three novices when he was desperate to join in a dog-fight below. At one moment he spotted three red Fokkers "sitting at about our level and east of the scrap." The two enemies observed one another, cruising "around and around." Were the Germans also there for the experience, or were they trying to lure the four British aircraft into a trap? Springs suspected the latter and kept his young charges under his wing.

On July 9, Callender got into another scrap with the Germans, one that cost the life of his flight commander, Arthur Claydon. Casualties were mounting, but replacements were arriving, one of whom was another American, John Donaldson, from Fort Yates, North Dakota. The son of Gen. Thomas Donaldson, the twenty-year-old was a graduate of Cornell University and a confident pilot who arrived at the squadron on July 3. He didn't have long have to acclimatize to his new surrounds; on July 14, 32 Squadron moved two hundred miles south to Touquin, a town on the Marne, east of Paris, where perhaps this time the great offensive might unfold.

They were ordered to carry out low level attacks on the Marne bridges and strafe enemy troops and artillery. Every heart in the squadron sunk, except Donaldson's, who had yet to become acquainted with the terror of low-level flying. On July 22 he scored his first victory, a Fokker D.VII shot down over Mont Notre

Some in 32 Squadron found John Donaldson brash, but all admitted he was a brilliant pilot.

Dame, the same dogfight in which Rogers finally got his name on the squadron scoreboard.

It had been a hell of a scrap, Rogers wrote his fiancée, erupting as they escorted a squadron of bombers on a raid over German positions. The dozen Fokkers hadn't spotted the S.E.5s flying above the bombers and they had "tumbled down on them like a load of bricks." Two "particularly gaudy" Fokkers caught Rogers's attention and he singled out one, giving him a couple of "good bursts at close range." The machine turned on its back, its pilots doomed to an appalling death. All in all, four Fokkers were downed, cause for celebration had it not been for an incident on the way home. One of the bombers took a direct hit from an A.A. battery. "It went down a mass of flames," wrote Rogers. "Not a pretty sight, especially as one of the chaps jumped out at about 12,000 ft."

It rained throughout July 23, one of those wet summer days that feel like February with the cloud so low one could almost reach up and touch it. The members of 32 Squadron decided on a whim to head into Paris in a seven-passenger Packard and live it up for the night.

It was one of the incongruities of a combat squadron; the ease with which they could replace austerity with comfort and forgo terror in favor of gratification. First the eight pilots dined at Maxim's, then they went to the Casino, which Rogers described as a "sort of combination theatre-café." Afterward, they strolled through the streets of Paris, marveling at the women, and telling each other that while the air war could be hell, it was still a darn sight better than life led by the "Poor Bloody Infantry" in the trenches.

CHAPTER 12

Why Are You Crying, Sir?

There was still no news of John McGavock Grider forty-eight hours after his failure to return from his patrol. Since his anguished entry in his diary the night of his friend's disappearance, Elliott Springs had convinced himself all was well. In a letter to his stepmother dated June 20 he wrote: "I imagine his motor cut out. I don't think Archie could have gotten him—I saw no Huns about—and I think I killed the observer so I don't believe Mac got hit [during the attack on the enemy aircraft]. . . . I feel sure that Mac is personally safe wherever he has landed. He's a prisoner all right but no one knows how I miss him. No man ever had a truer friend, and the fact we fought together and in unison and harmony shows the confidence we had in one another."

However, with each day that passed, Springs's hope receded. If Grider was a prisoner, word would reach the squadron, more often than not dropped on the aerodrome by a single German aircraft. But no messages fell from the sky. One message did arrive at the Grider plantation in Arkansas, delivered into the hands of John's father. It ran: "Lieutenant Grider reported missing in action June 18, 1918."

Springs contacted the Red Cross but they had no record of a John McGavock Grider; undeterred he arranged for the charity to send Grider some food parcels the moment they learned of his prison camp. Mac wasn't dead, Springs was sure of it. Anyone but Mac.

The Red Cross finally contacted Springs at the end of July. They had news from the Germans: a body had been identified as John McGavock Grider. The confirmation devastated Springs. He told his father about it in two short sentences, each one shackled by suppressed emotion. It was left to Captain B.A. Baker to write Grider's two children:

My Dear John and George:

I am writing to you to tell you of your father, who came out to France with us and who one day after flying for a long way over into the enemy's country, I am very sorry to say did not return; and whom, I am more sorry to tell you, neither you nor I will ever see him again. Your mother will read you this letter and I dare say there are many things in it you will not understand; but she will keep it for you and later you will be able to realize it more, and you will be able to see how fine a man he was. We came out to France in the middle of last May, a new squadron under a very famous leader. The pilots were carefully chosen and with us came three Americans, one of whom was your father. All of them were very keen and none more so than he. He was always cheerful and always out to hunt the Germans. He had several fights and with two or three other pilots helped to drive down several enemy machines. And then one day he went out, a cloudy day with a strong wind blowing from the west—blowing our machines over toward Germany. And he saw an enemy machine—a two-seater high up in the sky and about fifteen miles over. With another pilot he immediately made fast, keen only on bringing it down. They soon closed in on it and, after a short fight, down he shot the German. And then they both turned to come home, battling against the strong wind. After some time the guns from the ground opened fire, and the other pilot (also an American called Springs) lost sight of him and thought he was following, for it is often difficult to see other machines in the air. He (Springs) came home, but there was no sign of your father; we waited, hoping he had landed somewhere, but no news came, and we were forced to give him up as missing and could only hope that he was at least alive and a prisoner. But we were glad for a time that before he was lost he had brought down the German. Days went by and we hoped for news. And then one day it came through that he had fallen behind the enemy's lines. I can-not tell you how sorry we were, for we had lost a very great friend, a fine pilot and a very brave soldier. And you will hardly realize the greatness of your loss, but you will remember enough of him, and your mother will tell you of him, so that you will turn out in later years as fine men as he was; and you will remember with pride how nobly he fell in the war, which I hope by the time you are grown men will be finished once and for all. And so now I will say goodbye to both of you, hoping that you will cheer up and cheer up your mother too, because, like you, she too feels very sad indeed and it is up to you to try to help her forget her sadness. And so goodbye.

[Signed] B. A. Baker, Captain.

Grider's loss wasn't the only one endured by 85 Squadron in June 1918. Billy Bishop was recalled to England in the second half of the month at the request of the Canadian government. His luck couldn't last, they reasoned, if he kept hunting Germans on a daily basis. Sooner or later he would be shot down, and Canada wanted living heroes, not dead ones. He was ordered home to help organize the new Canadian Flying Corps. "This is ever so annoying," he wrote to his wife.

The squadron gave Bishop a send-off to remember. Springs was to the fore of the celebrations, as assistant mess president and "representative of Bacchus." Dinner was filet of sole, broiled chicken, and fresh peas, followed by strawberry ice cream, camembert, and coffee, all washed down with several bottles of wine of an excellent 1906 vintage.

With no Bishop and his replacement as squadron commander, the noted ace Mick Mannock, yet to arrive at St. Omer, Springs flew with less restraint than ever. On June 25, he spotted a German two-seater east of Kemmel. Springs left his patrol and dived on the enemy aircraft, confident this "cold meat" would take only a minute or so to destroy. "Not so," he wrote his father. "I had picked the wrong Hun." His adversary was, in RAF slang, "a stout fellow," and for several minutes the two aircraft dueled. "Just as I was about to open fire the Hun turned sharply to the left and I was doing about 200 [mph] I couldn't turn," wrote Springs. "So I pulled up and half rolled and came down on him again. He turned up to the right and forced me on the outside arc giving his observer a good shot at me as I turned back the other way to cut him off from the other side."

For a second Springs was the cold meat. If the observer had been good he would have dealt the American a fatal blow. But his shots went wide, and in an instant Springs pulled up, half rolled, and opened fire from above and behind. Still the German pilot tried to atone for the incompetency of his observer with a deft piece of flying: he stalled, side-stepped Springs, and allowed his gunner a second chance to end the fight. But Springs also had a clear shot and his burst hit his enemy's engine. The German was now in serious trouble—cold meat. He put his machine into a spin in a desperate attempt to escape his assassin. Springs followed him down, "firing at him from every conceivable angle and [I] even got so exasperated that I threw an ammunition drum at him."

The rest of the British patrol arrived to join in the kill, sending a "steady stream of lead into him." Springs turned away from the destruction at 1,000 feet. It was no longer fun. The pilot had deserved better.

Two days later Springs was out again on patrol, accompanied by Captain McGregor and a newcomer to the squadron, Lt. Donald Inglis. They encountered a German two-seater east of Bapaume, this time crewed with an observer who knew how to hit the target. McGregor led the attack, overshot, so Springs seized the initiative in feverish pursuit of that all-important fifth victory. He came "in close from an angle and got under him." His pressed his trigger finger but nothing happened. He pressed it again. Nothing. He became aware of tracer fire lacerating his wings, "like wood fire crackling, only more so."

Then his oil pressure went dead. "There was nothing to do but try and glide back to the lines," he recalled. As Springs slid slowly down from the sky, German anti-aircraft batteries opened up, and as he came nearer to earth, infantrymen joined in the fusillade with rifles and pistols. Springs even saw one soldier hurl a tin can in his direction. Then he saw the ground coming up, faster and faster. He covered his face with his hands and braced for the impact.

"Why are you crying, sir? You're back home."

It took Springs a few moments to recalibrate his senses. The voice wasn't German, it was definitely English. The American pointed to his mouth and gibbered, "My teeth! They're all gone!"

"No they're not, sir," said the British soldier. "Here they are."

He reached a hand inside Springs's mouth and pulled back his lips from his teeth. A field dressing was applied to the hole in his chin, and soon a padre arrived to pour cognac down his throat. By

Anti-aircraft fire was rarely fatal, but it could cause a lot of superficial damage to aircraft, as seen from this shredded upper wing.

evening Springs was a patient in the Duchess of Sutherland's hospital in St. Omer, clad in the red silk pajamas that he'd had on under his flying suit.

McGregor and Larry Callahan arrived at his bedside the next day, relieved to learn that apart from the hole in his chin, their comrade had nothing worse than a concussion. Callahan handed to

Captain Malcolm McGregor of 85 Squadron was a friend to the Three Musketeers.

the patient a "crocus sack full of champagne and we had a binge."
As they drank, Callahan promised he'd collect Springs's replacement
S.E.5 and fly it back to base so it would be waiting for him as soon as
he returned to the squadron.

However, when Callahan next visited Springs, he found his
friend in a foul temper, cursing at a telegram he clutched in his hand.
Springs had been appointed a flight commander in the 148th Aero
Squadron, one of two all-American squadrons, 17th Aero being the

A Flight of 148th Squadron: Wyly, Rabe, Kindley, Knox, and Creech.

other, attached to the RAF. "I want to stay with 85," Springs complained to Callahan, "where I am reasonably sure of getting some Huns and where all is going well."

Springs told Callahan he'd been on the phone to RAF headquarters to argue his case, only to be curtly informed that "I wasn't doing the appointing this season." Callahan suggested Springs should cable Washington to request the order be rescinded. It was a neat idea but it would take too long. They both knew how slowly the wheels of military bureaucracy turned. "It looks like I'll have to go [to the 148th Aero] though I can't figure why they would yank me away from 85 like this after all the trouble Major Bishop and Capt. Horn took to get me."

CHAPTER 13

I Am an Old Man

At the 3rd Aviation Instruction Center at Issoudun, two hundred miles south of 32 Squadron's base at Touquin, Lt. Arthur Taber wrote his father a long letter on July 7. He had been at the center three months and wanted his father to know why his aviation career appeared to have stalled. It was all because of his initial decision not to train as a fighter pilot. "I have analyzed minutely my attitude on this question and have come to the conclusion that my decision is based upon prudence and not upon cowardice," stated Taber. "I am certainly not afraid to go out as a chasse [fighter] pilot; on the contrary, it is so alluring a career that it would be easy to do; but my feeling is that it is my duty to gain all the experience possible so that I may later on be a better chasse pilot than now, and thus save for the government a pilot and his plane."

To validate his point, Taber chose the "striking example" of some of his classmates from Oxford. While there, he "lived with some Americans—all perfectly fine chaps and crazy to go chasse, like everybody else. Eighteen of them went to the front, and in six weeks there were six left. The fault was not with them, for there could not have been finer men, but they were not sufficiently experienced for such a tough job as chasse fighting. Three of them dived on *one* Hun machine with the result that they all collided and were killed, their planes utterly smashed, and the Hun escaped."[28]

---

[28] Records indicate that Taber was misinformed. At the time of his letter only Grider of the *Carmania* contingent had been killed and there had been no such collision involving three Americans.

Taber had hoped to become a reconnaissance pilot, but, he told his father, he was reconsidering. He was concerned that if the Germans should develop a "a plane which can overtake and shoot down the now supreme reconnaissance planes, I shall not be so keen upon going out on the latter type." Therefore, Taber said, he was having second thoughts about becoming a fighter pilot and might perhaps undertake the training after all.

Alas, a day after writing the letter, Taber was hauled out of flying school and assigned to duty as a transfer pilot. Not that he was crestfallen at the collapse of his ambition to fly fighters. It was, he declared, "the most extraordinary piece of good luck," and to cap it all he was based just outside Paris. As he told his father, he was now "contributing materially to the success of the present allied effort by keeping the squadrons at the front supplied with new planes."

Elliott Springs had also been busy writing letters. Time had been "hanging heavy" as he lay in the Duchess of Sutherland's hospital in St. Omer recovering from concussion and waiting for the wound in his chin to heal. He was also coming to terms with the fact he had but no choice to comply with the order instructing him to join 148th Aero Squadron.

On June 28, he propped himself up in bed and composed a long letter to Maj. Harold Fowler, liaison officer between the British and American forces. It was Fowler's job to best integrate the two all-American squadrons within the RAF, a role he doubtless found mundane given his experience as a combat pilot.

Born in Liverpool, England, in 1887, Fowler's family had moved to New York when he was a boy but he retained a strong sense of his British identity. After a spell working in the New York Stock Exchange, Fowler was appointed in 1913 as secretary to Walter Hines Page, the U.S. Ambassador to Great Britain. Within two years, however, Fowler was serving in the trenches as an artillery officer, but, like so many junior officers, the allure of the airplane proved too strong and he soon volunteered for the RFC. He flew combat missions throughout the "Bloody April" of 1917, earning a Military Cross for his "conspicuous gallantry and devotion to duty."

However, as soon as the United States entered the war, Fowler applied for a transfer, and his experience was put to good in the Aviation Section of the Signal Corps. On May 18, 1918, he replaced Maj. Thomas Bowen as liaison officer, an inspired appointment that

Lieutenant George Wise of 148th Squadron. *Library of Congress*

proved of enormous benefit to the incorporation of the 17th and
148th Aero Squadrons into the 65th Wing of the RAF.

"He therefore understood better than many Americans the
possibilities and the difficulties of British organization," wrote Lt.
Frederick Mortimer Clapp, the 17th's adjutant. "He saw, as no one

before him had in the slightest degree tried to see, the necessity of seconding us in the desire we entertained of making our relations with the British happy and friendly."

Fowler was like no other liaison officer. He used his own Sopwith Camel to fly from airfield to airfield, seeking out the American pilots flying with RAF squadrons, and allowing him to indulge his love of flying. It was a thankless task for much of the time. Not only were many of the pilots unhappy at being uprooted, but so were the squadron commanders who, by the summer of 1918, held their American pilots in the highest regard. They were, as one squadron noted, "the flower of the American fighting stock."

In Springs, Fowler knew he had one of America's finest combat pilots; wasn't that why Captain Morton Newhall, 148th's commander, had been adamant he wanted Springs in his squadron?

Fowler might very well have flown his Camel when he came to visit Springs in the Duchess of Sutherland's hospital, depositing some candy by his bedside, and then asking him to produce a memorandum on the principles of aerial combat.

The result was a detailed document that was as much an eulogy to 85 Squadron as anything else. Under Major Bishop, wrote Springs, they "worked on the principle that a scout patrol was ordered to perform a definite duty and this duty would be performed best by sticking closely to the job in hand and not by wandering about the skies indiscriminately in search of EA."

Springs's memo was surprisingly coherent considering his head was still heavy with concussion. His advice was just what Fowler wanted, pearls of wisdom to pass on to the inexperienced pilots.

- It is foolish to fight EA Scouts except when it is possible to start the fight from above.
- If the patrol leader does not lead the patrol down, individual pilots should not attack on their own.
- Great care should be taken in the morning when the sun is unfavorable [rising in the east, into the eyes of the RAF]. If you cannot attack with the advantage, don't attack.
- Daring without skill is not an asset but a serious menace.

Springs was released from the hospital the day after writing his memo, but instead of heading to 148th, he hitched a ride back to 85 Squadron and pleaded one last time to remain with them. But there was nothing

Young American recruits at one of the Texas training fields, circa 1918. *Library of Congress*

anyone could do. The appointment was official; he was now the commander of B Flight, 148 Aero Squadron, based at Capelle, three miles south of Dunkirk.

He arrived at his new base on the July 1, probably having been filled in by Fowler on the squadron's history. Formed the previous fall, the 148th did their initial training at Fort Worth, Texas, a base that had been laid out to British specifications. As a Texas newspaper, the *Bonham Daily Favorite*, explained in its edition of August 8, 1917, an official communique had been issued the previous day, which stated that Lt. H. B. Denton would be responsible for overseeing the construction of the training facility. "This camp in Texas will mean still closer cooperation between the aviation societies of the American and British forces and a further standardization of work," said Denton. "The plan is to reproduce in Texas aviation schools like those of Camp Borden. . . . [A] large number of the cadets recruited in New York will be sent to Texas to finish their training."

Fort Worth consisted of three fields to the north, south, and west. Locals knew them as Hicks, Benbrook, and Everman but the cadets designated them Camp Taliaferro, Field Nos. 1, 2, and 3. Flying conditions in Texas presented a particular challenge to the cadets, as in the Lone Star State the air was "much dryer and less buoyant [than in Europe]. Calm air was the exception, despite the comparatively flat country." In addition the temperature range at Fort Worth was extreme with the arrival of the "blue norther," a Texas phenomomen in which a fast-moving cold front causes temperatures to plummet, sometimes, as was the case in 1918, from 70 to 20 degrees Fahrenheit in a couple of hours.

On February 24, 1918, two days before the 148th shipped out to England on board RMS *Olympic*, the *Galveston Daily News* ran an article about Fort Worth. It began with a declaration that "the American youth has a natural aptitude for flying," and that over the winter the cadets in Texas "have proved almost startling to instructors from the allied armies who are here to give the Americans the advantage of their experience and knowledge."

Nonetheless such proficiency had a price, continued the paper, noting that the death on February 23 of Franklin Fairchild of Pelham, New York, brought to forty-seven the number of the cadets killed since Fort Worth began training recruits in October 1917. This was forty more fatalities than the American-run training facility in Houston, and the *Galveston Daily News* was curious to discover why Fort Worth, with its veteran British and Canadian instructors, should have racked up so many fatal accidents. An officer cadet explained that: "[t]he British theory is that the men should receive early instruction in all the difficult work they will have to do in actual service while the American trainers spend a larger part of their time in drilling the fundamentals of flying."

While American cadets flying under American instruction were forbidden from diving and looping and half-rolling, the British instructors had no such qualms about ordering their charges to perform such maneuvers. Partly this was because they were not subject to American military discipline and could not be punished for breaches of procedure, but also it was because the British and Canadian instructors were combat veterans. In the skies over France they had learned the hard way that the theory taught in warm classrooms by well-meaning

Kent Curtis was one of the Oxford cadets who later transferred to 148 Squadron.

but untested instructors was irrelevant in a dogfight. They preferred practical instruction, regardless of the danger that entailed.

After spending two weeks in England, the 148th arrived in France on March 17, 1918, and for the next few weeks shadowed 40 Squadron RAF "to learn something of the maintenance tasks involved in keeping a flying squadron airworthy."

Springs's chagrin at being plucked from 85 Squadron diminished when he arrived at Capelle and saw some familiar faces—men he'd last seen at Oxford, what now seemed a lifetime ago. These included Kent Curtis, Bill Clements, Linn Foster, and John Fulford, not to mention Henry Clay, and Bennett Oliver.

Oliver was the son of a former senator of Pennsylvania whose first trip in an airplane had been a Thanksgiving joyride in 1916. Climbing out of the Curtiss Jenny cockpit on Governor's Island after a flight around New York, Oliver exclaimed: "This is for me!" In May 1917 he began flight instruction, and three months later he was one of the fifty-two cadets aboard RMS *Aurania* under the command of Capt. Geoffrey Dwyer.

He had been one of the handful of Americans posted to 84 Squadron in May 1918, and over the course of the weeks and months that followed he'd learned much about the war in the air. The majority of German pilots, he believed, were short on "initiative and guts." He told his new comrades in 148th Squadron that he had "never had a fight on our side of the lines" because the enemy were too scared to cross into enemy territory. Bennett was also dismissive about the German aircraft; although he admitted the Fokker D.VII was good, the Albatros lacked agility because of its "heavy slow speed and six cylinder engine," and the Pfalz was "pretty slow." He did admire the Germans for one thing, though: "they used smoke tracers which left a trail so that if you saw the shots go to the left, you simply turned to the right and vice versa." Oliver ("Bim" to Springs) was appointed leader of A Flight, Henry Clay took responsibility for C Flight, and Springs was in charge of B Flight.

Just as he was getting to know his new squadron, Springs fell ill. It was, he wrote home a fortnight later, a combination of factors: a toxic mix of "whiskey, brandy, anti-tetanus serum, and morphine." Nothing to worry about, though, even if his eyes were bad and his joints swelled up to twice their size. Larry Callahan dropped in to see his fellow Musketeer, filling Springs in about his second victory and about life in 85 Squadron. Springs wanted all the news, and listened agog as Callahan told him they'd shot down twenty Germans since the beginning of July for the loss of just two men. "It makes me sick to think what I've missed," Springs wrote his father.

Henry Clay was another Oxford cadet.

Discharged from hospital on July 19, Springs was sent on leave to Paris for a few days, but he spent most of the time feeling like "a ham sandwich at a banquet." He ate well, and drank much, but neither activity brought him much joy. He stared listlessly at the beautiful women gliding along the sidewalks of the French capital, but they too failed to arouse much interest. His thoughts were at the front. He wanted to be back with the boys; that's where he was happiest. He sat at a café and wrote to his stepmother. "I am an old man," he began. "The mirror shows no white hairs but mental reflections shows unmistakable signs of old age."

He was back with the 148th by the end of July. "I feel much better," he told his stepmother on July 30, the day he was chased home by a couple of Fokkers. However, he still clung to 85 Squadron like a child to its mother's apron strings. He phoned Larry Callahan each day, congratulating his friend on taking his tally to four. But there was also bad news. The squadron's new C.O., the great British ace, Mick Mannock, had been shot down and killed.

The next day, July 31, Springs celebrated his birthday. Callahan and Spencer Horn flew up from 85 Squadron for a birthday lunch and they spent much of the meal discussing the dead. Springs learned that Mannock had died in the way he'd always feared—shot down in flames—and Callahan brought confirmation that Grider's remains had been formally identified.

Springs was now twenty-two, but there were days when he felt twice that age.

CHAPTER 14

Low-Level Terror

By the beginning of August 1918, the Allies had just under two thousand fighter aircraft concentrated on the Western Front: ten times fewer than the number recommended by some within the RAF, but still six times more fighters than the German air force possessed. In fact, the RAF had undergone a massive expansion in the preceding two years. In 1916, the RFC, as it then was, had only 6,633 machines in total; that figure had more than doubled to 14,832 the following year; and by 1918 the RAF had 30,782 aircraft of varying types.

The 1,900 fighter aircraft assembled by the Allies in the high summer of 1918 represented the largest air operation of the war. They would play a crucial part in the impending offensive, which would become known as the Battle of Amiens. On July 24, a conference of national army commanders—Field Marshal Philippe Pétain of France, Britain's Field Marshal Douglas Haig, and Gen. John Pershing of the American Expeditionary Forces—met to discuss the strategy for the rest of the year and into 1919. No one believed the war would be won quickly, but all sensed that Germany was weakening: a prize fighter who had given it his best shot but to no avail, and was now on the back foot, with heavy legs and hopeless eyes.

The conference was chaired by Field Marshal Ferdinand Foch, commander in chief of the Allied Forces in France, who stated that their objective in the forthcoming offensive was to "embarrass the enemy in the utilization of his reserves and not allow him sufficient time to fill up his units." Sir Henry Rawlinson's Fourth Army would lead the attack, the British troops—complemented by Canadian and Australian divisions—assaulting twenty thousand Germans

Facilities were rudimentary at airfields in France, as seen at this unknown base. *Library of Congress*

positioned at Amiens, on the Somme River, where in March the British had been so humiliatingly overrun.

The first inkling 32 Squadron had of the offensive was an order to move from Touquin, in the French sector, to Bellevue in the British zone. It was the squadron's fifth move in two months, enough to cause even the most stoic of ground crew to curse the top brass as he loaded up the trucks for the 130-mile trip north.

Bogart Rogers was lucky. He missed this move, writing his fiancée on August 2 (the day before 32 relocated to Bellevue) about his furlough in London. He was staying at the National Hotel in the heart of the British capital, and the previous evening had dined with one of his classmates from flying school in Canada. Rogers was emphatic that it had just been the two of them; old friends, both male. Isabelle had expressed her concern in a previous letter about the temptations her Bo might encounter in London or Paris. She had heard such tales. "I'm glad you mentioned the women, Isabelle," wrote Rogers. "A great many fellows come on leave, don't know anyone, haven't any particular interests, and get into trouble. It isn't hard to do. But Izzy, if war doesn't do one other thing, it teaches you the real worth of a decent woman."

Alvin Callender had yet to be exposed to the temptations of degenerate Britain but he soon would be; his two-week furlough was scheduled for the second half of August, and he wrote his sister on August 4 to tell her what he had planned—a tour of their ancestral home, Scotland, with the first few days spent visiting Edinburgh.

He had a few harsh words for his sister, ordering her to "quit telling me to be an 'ace.'" There were only four aces in the RAF, he told her, and they were found in a pack of cards. Then, Callender softened his tone and described the squadron's new home, so close to the frontline that the guns made it hard to sleep at night. But she wasn't to worry, he added; "the worst three months is over now as far as air work is concerned." Fall wasn't far off, and the weather would keep the Hun out of the sky. Callender reckoned the war would be over "by the winter of 1919," and in the meantime he was enjoying life and appreciating the eclectic personalities in the officers' mess. "In the squadron now we have 6 Englishmen, 2 Scotchmen, 1 Irishman, 7 Canadians, 6 Americans, 2 Australians, and 1 South African," he explained. "Pretty nearly every breed of white man there is, isn't it?"

One of the six Americans was a recent arrival, Lt. Frank Lucien Hale, "Bud" to his friends, who hailed from a prosperous family in Fayetteville, New York, but who considered himself more of a Syracuse boy. The twenty-three-year-old arrived at 32 Squadron with the name of the city painted on the fuselage of his S.E.5a air-craft. He also walked through the door of the mess with the unmistakable air of a

Lieutenant Frank Lucien Hale, "Bud" to his friends, became an ace with 32 Squadron.

man who knew what he wanted from life. This single-mindedness had taken Hale in the space of two years from a driver with the 4th Ambulance Company of Syracuse on the Mexican border in 1916 to an officer pilot in the RAF. Hale's forceful personality had "made life interesting for the company's officers" in the Ambulance Company and they were mightily relieved when, on arriving back from Mexico, he left the unit to become a pilot in the Aviation Corps. But Hale was in for a shock. Presenting himself at the recruiting station, he was informed that his "lack of a college education was an insurmountable bar."

Outraged, Hale traveled to Washington and browbeat high officials until they "agreed to waive the four years in college." One hurdle was surmounted, but the next proved impossible to overcome, even for a man of Hale's ambition. He failed the equilibrium test on account, so he said to his family and friends when he returned home, of a kick in the head from a horse when a child. Hale was "crestfallen," his dreams of becoming a pilot in ruins. However, he didn't stay whipped for long. He learned of the long road to Canada, and in 1917 enlisted in the RFC. A serious injury sustained in a crash during take-off, a result of engine failure, postponed his graduation, but, by the summer of 1918, Hale was in England, waiting to be posted to France.

A blanket of gray mist greeted the dawn on August 8, 1918, a date later described by Ludendorff as "the black day of the German army." Within a few hours the British Fourth Army had thrust through the German positions with the same exultant ferocity as Ludendorff's troops had displayed five months earlier. The gap smashed in the German lines was fifteen miles long, and Kaiser Wilhelm II soon realized that his soldiers had "reached the limits of our capacity." Ludendorff knew also the war was now lost, but both he and his monarch agreed to fight on in the hope of strengthening the bargaining position when the inevitable surrender came.

The rapidity of the Fourth's advances caught everyone unawares—officers, infantrymen, and airmen. Reconnaissance aircraft were soon reporting that all roads to the Somme were clogged with demoralized enemy soldiers. Consequently, "existing bombing arrangements were cancelled and a maximum effort directed towards destroying the Somme bridges." There were fourteen road and rail bridges between Bray and Pithon, but they were just the permanent structures.

By late summer 1918, Kaiser Wilhelm II (center) knew the war was lost, as did his generals, Hindenburg (left) and Ludendorff. *Library of Congress*

German engineers had also improvised numerous temporary bridges to facilitate the flight of their troops and supplies.

At 1:45 p.m., twelve aircraft from 32 Squadron were ordered to bomb Béthencourt Bridge, but heavy ground fire staved off the British attack. Like a swarm of angry hornets, the S.E.5s sought out other targets, strafing columns of enemy troops and dropping their bombs on A.A. batteries. Later in the day they returned to Béthencourt, a six-strong flight containing Callender and a nineteen-year-old Canadian called Walter Gilbert.[29]

They dropped their bombs firstly on the north-east end of the bridge, then its middle, and then Gilbert made one final pass, coming in impossibly low, his Sopwith pockmarked with small arms fire, and dropping his load on the approach to the bridge. The flight returned

[29] After the war Gilbert made a name for himself as an aerial explorer, mapping large swaths of the Arctic coastline.

to Bellevue, replenished their bombs, and took off once more for Béthencourt. A second flight joined the raid, among their number John Donaldson, but still their target bridged the Somme, damaged but too strong to be destroyed by a deluge of 25-pound Cooper bombs.

Breaking off the attack, Donaldson spotted a flight of five Fokker D.VIIs headed their way. He and two other Sopwiths accepted the odds, and engaged the enemy over the town of Licourt, Donaldson leading the assault with a frontal attack on the German leader. "Firing about fifty rounds without result, [I] then made a climbing turn and dived on a second enemy machine, firing 100 rounds at him, at very close range," he wrote later in his report of the dogfight. The German fell "into a straight dive and crashed to earth, midway between Licourt and Morcham where it remained with its tail vertical."

Donaldson's victim was one of sixty-five enemy aircraft shot down on August 8, for the loss of forty-five RAF machines. In truth, however, the British had lost far more machines with a further fifty-two aircraft returning across the lines so badly damaged they were no longer airworthy. In all, almost twenty five percent of Allied aircraft on low-level flying missions were put out of commission on August 8.

Certainly the belligerence of the Germans had surprised the RAF, more used to the enemy waiting for the fight to come to them. Different tactics were deployed on August 9, with many fighter squadrons instructed to leave the bridge raids to bomber squadrons. No. 32 Squadron were involved in an attack on a bridge at Falvy but two German *Jastas* were patrolling the sector. The sky darkened with aircraft as the battle was joined. Donaldson claimed his fourth victory, a flamer at 12,000 feet, but then his own aileron was shot away from a burst from his rear. A fellow American, Reuben Paskill, saved the life of his compatriot by chasing the Fokker away, but Donaldson was out of the fight. Callender and another pilot took on three Germans over Villers, but thick cloud made it hard to score a clear kill.

The cloud had dropped even lower by late afternoon when 32 Squadron provided an escort to bombers from 49 Squadron. In the murk, the bombers became separated from their chaperone, and were attacked by the twenty Fokkers. Some of the S.E.5s managed to grope their way through the clouds to come to the bombers' rescue, but in the ensuing mêlée Paskill was shot down and killed.

The following day brought no respite for the RAF. Although its army was on the retreat, Germany's air force was moving in the other direction, including the famous *Jagdgeschwader* 1, now commanded by Hermann Göring, following the death of Manfred von Richthofen and his successor, Wilhelm Reinhard.

Although Donaldson and Callender both scored their fifth victories (the former beating the latter to the accolade of ace by a mere ten minutes during the same dogfight), 32 Squadron lost another pilot—Lt. Peter Macfarlane, a twenty-three-year-old Scot—while another was shot down and captured.

Two days later, Callender finally had a chance to write home. The bitter fighting of the past week had earned the Germans a new-found respect in the American's eyes. They no longer ran from a fight. "We have a good way to go yet before we fight over German territory," he told his mother. He said little of his own experiences, preferring

Wilhelm Reinhard had also led *Jagdgeschwader* 1 before his death in action.

to look forward to his forthcoming leave. Not long to go now. Callender would be off across the Channel just as soon as Bogart Rogers returned from his furlough in "Blighty," as the British called home.

Rogers reached Bellevue on August 14. It took a while for him to come to terms with the many changes: not just the new airfield, but the new faces, and the new German tactics. Rube Paskill's death hit Rogers hard. The two had been friends. But, on the bright side, he wrote his fiancée, Wilfred Green and Sturley Simpson had both been decorated for gallantry. Rogers had run an eye over the clutch of new pilots and three "are very good, have all been instructors in Canada, can surely fly, and are regular fellows besides."

One of the three was Hale, already blooded in battle despite the fact he'd been at the front barely more than a week. The era of easing new pilots gently into combat was long gone. There was no time for that now, not if the RAF wanted to take control of the sky. Hale's first letter home had been written on August 13, the brio of the newcomer's prose matching the zeal in his eyes. "We have had only two real scraps so far since I arrived," he wrote. "I managed to get back safely but have no Huns to my credit so far."

Hermann Göring assumed command of *Jagdgeschwader* 1 following the death of Manfred von Richthofen.

He described his first dogfight, how the guns of an enemy Fokker sound like "a riveting hammer," and then turned to his own S.E.5a. "Breaking in a new airplane is like breaking in a new auto. The engine has to be nursed along for 20 or 30 hours before it can be run at top speed. It seems great to have my own machine, and I surely am in love with it. I tell you, when everything depends on you and your machine, a fellow is bound to know, absolutely, what the machine can and will do in an emergency."

The men in the squadron weren't bad either. He mentioned that he knew five of them from RFC training in Canada the previous fall—Callender, Jerry Flynn, Harry Carson, John Trusler, and Montague Tancock, the latter an American from New Jersey. "We live like real men and have real fun, too," he said. "It is great out here. . . . [B]elieve me, if a fellow survives this war, he will have some thrilling experiences to tell."

Hale ended his letter with a throwaway sentence about a recent German air raid. From his account he'd hardly looked up from his armchair. His parents had enough to worry about without the thought their boy could be blown to bits as he sat reading the paper in the squadron mess. It was Rogers who gave a more detailed account of the raid to his fiancée. The squadron had just finished dinner when suddenly the airfield klaxon sounded and the lights in the mess went out. Pilots stopped talking and glanced skywards, or nervously at one another. Up above they "could hear the peculiar drone of a couple of Huns." For a couple of minutes the bombers circled the area and then "suddenly dropped some parachute flares. Fortunately they weren't right over us, for they light the whole place up like day." The Germans were after the town, not the airfield, but now the British anti-aircraft guns opened up and for several minutes "the usual Fourth of July celebration followed."

Lothar von Richtofen, brother of Manfred, survived the war but died in a flying accident in the 1920s.

If Allied air losses had been heavy in the days following the launch of the Fourth Army offensive, the damage inflicted upon the German air force was catastrophic. The Richthofen Circus lost thirty-nine of its fifty aircraft, and among the casualties was the high-ranking ace Lothar von Richthofen, brother of the Red Baron, badly wounded in action on August 12, probably a victim of American Capt. Field Kindley of the 148th Aero Squadron.

No. 32 Squadron was no longer subjected to the same intense low-level work of early August, but the second half of the month brought frequent patrols and escort assignments. Already Hale's letters had lost some of their ardor. First there was the heat, he complained to his parents, and the flies, too, "so thick that sleep is quite impossible." And he craved sleep. "Day before yesterday we had two patrols, and yesterday we had three. First at 5 A.M., second at 11:30 A.M., and third at 5 P.M. Each one lasted more than two hours. I was absolutely dead tired last night. Six hours of flying at 18,000 ft, or higher, and all the time dodging Archie, and expecting to meet some Hun machines, is no easy job I state." He mentioned that his ears were "ringing like a dozen church bells tonight" on account of the altitude, and then

Captain Field Kindley was an ace with the 148th Aero Squadron.

admitted he lacked the energy to write any more. "Have to get up at 5 o'clock in the morning."

On the morning of August 25, 32 Squadron provided an escort for a bombing raid "so far over the line that I shiver every time I think about it." Rogers then hurriedly ended his letter to Isabelle Young, telling her "this afternoon we're doing a nastier show. I can't go into details but it's a retaliation affair and the worth the effort involved."

The attack was a revenge strike for an air raid the previous evening on Bertangles, the aerodrome shared by 48 and 84 Squadrons. George Vaughn and Alex Matthews of the latter had been invited "across the railway tracks" to a concert party laid on by 48 Squadron. The pair were sat side by side enjoying the show when "a bomb dropped without warning squarely on the adjacent hangar full of Bristol fighters, starting a fire." Other bombs followed, and people jumped from their seats, fleeing for their lives. "Alex ran one way and I another," wrote Vaughn. "I fell into a bomb crater, immediately followed by several other people still in their performers' costumes."

The raid lasted several long minutes and when the last raider had vanished into the darkness, the survivors emerged from their hiding places to survey the damage. "Alex had been hit by machine gun fire from one of the bombers and had been instantly killed," wrote Vaughn. "There were many casualties among the personnel of the 48th."

By early evening on August 25, the bombing raid was underway and 32 Squadron were patrolling the skies in the vicinity of Hancourt, approximately ten miles northwest of Saint-Quentin. A flight of thirteen Fokker D.VIIs were spotted approaching the RAF bombers. Donaldson swooped on four blue-gray enemy aircraft and picked out one as his sixth victim. A long burst of one hundred rounds ripped through the colorful fuselage and the machine "went into a sideslip-dive, and after falling about 2,000 feet, the left wing of the enemy aircraft broke off." Donaldson watched with cold interest as the pilot leapt from his cockpit. Suddenly the American started. A parachute had blossomed and the German was floating gently down to earth.[30]

Hale had followed Donaldson into the fray, firing one hundred rounds into one of the other three Fokkers at very close range. "E.A. immediately turned over on its back, and went down into a spiral dive," Hale wrote in his combat report. "Pilot followed it down, observing it to crash about 2 miles East of an aerodrome, on side of road at Hancourt."

Hale was delighted. When he first joined the squadron he'd had reservations, heard rumors that 32 wasn't up to that much. "This hasn't been such a very good squadron up to now," he wrote his parents, "but we are going to try to buck it up a bit, and make it a crack squadron."

By "we," Hale probably meant those who had arrived from North America. One of them, Donaldson, was certainly creating a name for himself. On August 29, he took his tally to seven E.A. in thirty-eight days and on September 1, he anticipated adding an eighth to his score card when the squadron were ordered to provide an escort to a long-range bombing mission.

The British were faced with a strong westerly wind, a clear advantage to the Germans, who would be able to attack the British when they were laboring into the wind on the way back home low on fuel. (In a letter home Frank Hale said of one mission on a westerly wind that "it took us less than 20 minutes to go over but one hour and 45 minutes to come back.") Sure enough, that was when the Germans struck. Donaldson's A Flight, providing close escort, became separated from the top cover and were set upon by seven Fokkers. Montague Tancock managed to down one enemy aircraft, but Lieutenant Sandys-Winsch was wounded and neither Donaldson nor another American, Lt. Edwin Klingman, an insurance clerk from Greensboro before the war, returned to Bellevue. Someone claimed to have seen Donaldson shooting down his

---

[30] Germany had started issuing parachutes—known as *Heinecke Fallschirme, or* Heinecke parachutes—to its aircraft pilots in early 1918. Approximately twenty-one inches in diameter, the conical parachutes were made from silk, and static-line operated. The first pilot to use a parachute in combat was a member of *Jasta* 56 who, on April 1, 1918, leapt clear of his flaming Albatros.

eighth German before being forced to the ground by damage to his own aircraft.[31]

Frank Hale's guns had jammed in the first few seconds of the fight and in a letter home he described the unenviable position he found himself in. "The clouds were quite thick at about 3,000 feet so I dived into them. The two Huns were quite persistent and evidently thought that they would get me. I flew due east in the clouds, going further into Hunland all the time. Suddenly I came into the open. They started shooting everything at me from the ground. . . . I tried to spoil their aim by stunting, but couldn't. Then I dived into another cloud. They just filled this with Archie and flaming onions . . . so down I went to within a few feet of the ground and headed for our lines. For 10 or 12 miles I contour chased. Every time I would get anywhere within sight or range of a machine gun they shot at me. Finally I reached our lines, and you can't imagine what a relief it was. I certainly said a prayer of thanks to God for getting me out of that scrape."[32]

Two days later, 32 Squadron was out on a routine patrol in the early afternoon. No one expected trouble, they wouldn't be up for long, just a quick sortie over the line. Three miles over, "a dozen Fokkers appeared from nowhere." They dived on the flight commander, Jerry Flynn, the small Canadian with the lionheart, who had as his shadow a new pilot, young Canadian 2nd Lt. Frederick Pacey, a teacher from Ontario in civilian life. The pair were shot down in flames before the rest of the patrol could come to their rescue.

The squadron was stunned. Flynn's best friend, the veteran Wilfred Green, was hysterical when he landed. "Poor little Jerry!" he screamed. "Oh my God! They got him in flames." He blamed himself. "I let him down! I didn't protect him."

His fellow pilots tried to calm him. Consoling arms were draped around Green's shoulder but Rogers said "everyone was on the verge of tears. It was too great a tragedy to conceal. It penetrated their calloused exteriors and jabbled at their hearts."

The men retired to their quarters, lay on their beds, trying to get out of their head the image of Flynn's machine parceled in flame.

---

[31] Klingman survived the war, returned to his insurance company, and died of a heart attack in 1941 at the age of forty-five.

[32] "Flaming onions" was what British pilots christened the 37mm shells fired by the German five-barrel revolving antiaircraft gun. The shells could reach altitudes of 5,000 feet.

There was a febrile atmosphere at dinner that night. Rogers said "more cocktails than usual" had been served before they sat down. People were drinking to forget. "But for once they didn't work . . . they only made matters worse." Rogers later wrote an account of what followed:

> By the time the soup appeared everyone was three sheets to the wind but the teetotalers. There were guests for dinner and champagne was in order on guest nights. They guzzled it like water but it had no effect— the place was a morgue. Nobody talked—nobody dared talked. Jerry's seat was vacant, there wasn't a soul who would occupy it. It happened suddenly. A kid named John Trusler, grabbed his champagne glass, hurled it the length of the mess, leaped to his feet and started a vivid impression of a lunatic. . . . [H]e swore and cursed and cried. He cursed God and the Germans. He cursed the war and the army. He cursed his parents because he was born. He told Little Jerry Flynn—who he knew was sitting in the room listening to him, who was sitting right there in that chair—that he didn't have to worry. They couldn't kill him and get away with it. . . . [T]hey tried to stop him, and finally pulled him down into a chair. He hid his head in his hands and sobbed horribly. Half of the fellows were bawling. The rest were trying to quiet things down but feeling no better than the weepers.

The next morning, Flynn was just a statistic, a name in the squadron's lengthening roll of honor. Everyone, recalled Rogers, climbed into their cockpits having slipped on their "hard-boiled masks." Trusler grinned sheepishly when ribbed for his outburst. Green went off on patrol as sanguine as the rest, but once in the air, something seized possession of his mind. He landed a broken man. Gentle hands eased him out of the cockpit, this brave man whose "nerves snapped with the twang of a broken flying wire." Green was invalided back to England, never to fly again in combat, just as Callender returned from leave and was appointed Flynn's replacement as C Flight Commander.

CHAPTER 15

The 17th
Aero Squadron

For such an unprepossessing individual, Orville Ralston had a rare distinction. He had been among the eight Canada-trained aviators who marched into Fort Worth on October 17, 1917, the first recruits into the 17th Aero Squadron.

Ralston was from Nebraska. Born in September 1894, he graduated from the Nebraska State Normal School (now Peru State Teachers College) and was in the second year of studying dentistry at the University of Nebraska when he decided to enlist. Ralston was stout with protruding ears and wavy brown hair. At university he answered to the name of "Wob" on account of his wobbling walk; in the military he was "Tubby."

Ralston's formative years had been quiet and unexceptional; he'd been one of those boys content to stay in the background, undistinguished and unnoticed by many of his peers. However, that changed when he was among the first Aviation Corps recruits to be transferred to the RFC in Canada.

Upon arriving in Toronto, Ralston wrote home: "It seemed rather strange to be the first 'Yanks' in Canada. I know I felt embarrassed at the way in which we were watched by the cadets as well as the public in general."

Ralston was a natural pilot. On the ground he had an uneven gait, but once in the air he flew his machine with a singular smoothness. He was appointed commander of Flight C of the 17th Squadron when they began flying at Hicks Field, and in his letters home he described how he was growing accustomed to his newfound status. "People in Texas had never seen airplanes before," he wrote in his diary. "Hundreds would come out, flock around the machines, whenever we would land near a town. Often we had meals out and met many swell girls."

The hospitality of Fort Worth citizens toward aviation cadets became legendary. They subscribed $75,000 "to provide funds for the local branch of the American War Service Board, and rented a large club room and dancing hall in the center of the city, where comfortable accommodation was found for men of both the American and British services." The town's assorted ladies' clubs organized dances and the Fort Worth branch of the Y.M.C.A. "saw to it that commodious huts and writing rooms were furnished."

Jesse Creech was one of the first eight recruits to the 17th Squadron in 1917.

Ralston committed the name of the first eight cadets in the 17th to his diary: as well as himself there were Walter Jones, Ralph Gracie, Charles France, Ralph Snoke, Oliver Johnson, Harold Shoemaker, and Jesse Creech. They were soon joined by another eight recruits, and throughout the rest of the fall more young men arrived in Texas.[33]

Ralston was commissioned first lieutenant on December 31, 1917, nine days before the 17th Aero Squadron shipped out to England on board the *Carmania*, the same vessel that had conveyed the Three Musketeers to Europe four months earlier.

The 17th Aero Squadron arrived at an RFC rest camp at Romsey, Hampshire, in the south of England, radiating pride. They

---

[33] Of the first sixteen aviators to join the 17th Aero Squadron, seven were killed in the war and two became aces.

considered themselves the elite of American aviators; however, to the British, they were just fresh meat. "17th is split up," wrote Ralston in his diary on February 19, as dismayed as the rest of the squadron at their fate. They had enlisted together, trained together, and they wanted to fight together, but the British had long since dispensed with military sentimentality.

The Americans were ordered to France, and once there the British cleaved the squadron, assigning Headquarters Flight to 24 Squadron at Martigny; A Flight to 84 Squadron, at Guizancourt; B Flight to 60 Squadron, at Sainte-Marie-Cappel on the Flanders front; and C Flight to 56 Squadron at Baizieux.

For the first few months in France "the flights were totally out of touch with one another," recalled 1st Lt. Frederick Mortimer Clapp, who replaced Lt. Henry Bangs as squadron adjutant in the spring. The initial disquiet of the Americans at their treatment soon vanished when they realized this was all part of their instruction, and far more productive than attending some tedious flight school in Scotland. They were, wrote Clapp, "most exciting times" and the "men of the 17th Squadron learned much more than the mere care of their machines. They knew now what it meant to send out patrols and move incessantly from one aerodrome to another at the same time."

Orville Ralston was absent from this invaluable schooling. Since he was one of the squadron's ablest pilots, he had been kept behind in England to learn how to fly bombers. To Ralston it felt like a punishment. He wanted to fly fighters, and he confessed to his diary that he was "rather discouraged" at the unexpected turn of events. He began flying bombers—the DH.4 and "the deadly DH.9" (deadly to the pilots not the enemy on account of its unreliable engine)—and kept alive his dream of flying into combat inside a Camel or S.E.5. However, the news from France deepened his gloom. In June the 17th Aero Squadron began to reassemble at Petite Synthe aerodrome, recently vacated by Maj. Billy Bishop's 85 Squadron. On June 21 the squadron—assigned to the RAF's 65th Wing under the command of Lt. Col. Jack Cunningham—appointed as its commander Sam Eckert, who had performed well with 84 Squadron. Eckert's three flight commanders, in charge of A, B, and C respectively, were Mort Newhall, Weston Goodnow, and Lloyd Hamilton.

Hamilton was notified of his appointment on June 20, and a day later he arrived at Petite Synthe accompanied by Lt. Bill Tipton.

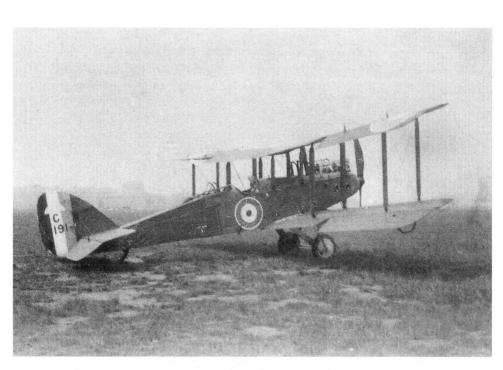

The DH.9 bomber was nicknamed "deadly" to British pilots on account of its unreliable engine.

Between them, while serving with 3 Squadron, they had shot down seven enemy aircraft in two months; Hamilton accounted for five to make him the first of the 150 "Warbirds" to become an ace. Tipton was soon promoted to take charge of B Flight, while Goodnow became A Flight commander in place of Newhall, appointed commanding officer of 148th Squadron.

Many of the pilots serving in the three flights had been shipped out with the 17th Squadron in January, including Ralph Gracie and Ralph Snoke, two of the cadets who had arrived at Fort Worth with Ralston. Others came "from the Training Brigade through the pool from which all British trained pilots were drawn."

However, a squadron of combat novices wouldn't survive long, so a nucleus of experienced pilots were transferred from the RAF squadrons they'd been flying in for months. Lieutenant Frank Dixon recalled that, on June 25, after scarcely a month with 209 Squadron, he and three fellow Americans were ordered to leave for 17th Aero Squadron. Henry Frost arrived at Petite Synthe from 210 Squadron, with whom he'd been flying since April 2; Merton Campbell turned up looking lost, bemused as to why after nearly four months of loyal service with 54 Squadron he'd been so abruptly uprooted.

To guard against the growth of resentment among his combat veterans, Sam Eckert adroitly nurtured an *espirit de corps* in the new squadron. An insignia was designed, "a white dumb-bell painted on each side of the fuselage aft of the cockpit" carried on all the 17th Squadron's 114 Sopwith Camels.[34]

Eckert also dispatched some personnel to the Channel port of Calais to buy luxuries for their quarters at Petite Synthe. They returned laden with "all the light-green iron garden chairs the Nouvelles Gaieties of that place possessed. . . . [W]icker chairs and cushions were bought too." Prints and pictures were hung from the walls of the mess, a piano was procured, along with a gramophone, and a stack of records, including Grieg's "Asa's Death" and the "Song of the Boatmen on the Volga."

Eckert also insisted that although the 17th was an exclusively American squadron, and proud of it, it would honor the influence of its ally. "British-trained, we retained their customs at mess," reflected Frank Dixon. "Dress without Sam Browne belts and waited for the C.O. to test the soup, although we failed to pass the port and drink to the King after dinner as the British did."

Frederick Clapp, the 17th's adjutant, recalled that the mess was a riotous place, reverberating with laughter most of the time as the pilots gleefully waited for some unfortunate pilot to arrive at dinner wearing his belt, or to light up a cigar before Eckert had a put a match to his own. "Nothing brought forth such peals of merriment as the infraction, through thoughtlessness, of any of our rules," wrote Clapp. "The offender bought drinks or cigars or both all around, depending upon the gravity of his crime, to shouts of 'Randolph, Randolph, take an order!'"

Like other pilots in the squadron, Dixon had a "tailor-made U.S. uniform from Burberry's . . . [but] used an off-the-rack British tunic with tie and shirt for work."

For the first couple of weeks of its existence at Petite Synthe, the 17th familiarized itself with its sector and aircraft. "The air was always full of the roar of engines on a fair day, and even on days when mists hung about the plains or clouds rolled up from the south and west,

---

[34] The 148th's emblem was a white triangle.

there was a roar at least from the test bench," remembered Clapp. "We watched the big bombing formations of the 211th take off in front of the hangars—twelve, fourteen, even sixteen D.H.9s getting away, one after the other, and disappearing into the haze toward Calais to get their height."

The 17th Aero Squadron crossed the lines for its first offensive patrol on July 15. Five days later it claimed its inaugural victory when Lt. Rodney Williams shot down a Fokker D.VII just east of Ostend. Later that day a congratulatory message was received from General Salmond, commanding the RAF in the field. "It was a great day with us and the enlisted men were quite as excited as the officers," wrote Clapp. "It meant much that at last, after so many discouragements and changes, we had achieved the beginning of our offensive career."

A party was held in the mess on the evening of July 20, an occasion tempered somewhat by the news that Lt. George Glenn from Virginia had become the squadron's first fatality after being shot down by a Fokker.

Lieutenant Rodney Williams shot down a Fokker D.VII on July 20, 1918, to claim 17th Squadron's first kill.

Lloyd Hamilton had missed the party in Williams's honor. He'd been sent on leave to London a few days earlier, but by the start of August he was back, a day after Robert Todd recorded the squadron's second victory.

On August 7, the day before the British Fourth Army launched their big offensive in Amiens, Hamilton and Merton Campbell were on an offensive patrol over Armentières. The pair were flying at 16,000 feet when they spotted a patrol of eight German Fokkers 8,000 feet lower. Refreshed after two weeks in London, Hamilton dove on his enemy with relish. "I settled on the tail of one Fokker and fired 200 rounds into him as he spiraled down," he wrote in his combat report. "I followed him down to 5,000 feet at which point a cloud of black smoke issued from his cockpit and he went down in an extremely steep spiral through a cloud, apparently completely out of control." Hamilton emerged from the cloud straight into the

Robert Todd claimed the squadron's second German a few days later.

path of a second Fokker. The German fired; Hamilton climbed, turned, and came out behind his prey. He sent a stream of bullets into the aircraft. "As he dove away, Lieut. Campbell came in on one side and then on to his tail, firing several bursts," wrote Hamilton. "I saw E.A. crash into a green field just east of Armentières. Lieut Campbell was at about 1,000 feet and I was at 500, both getting badly machine-gunned. When I was going toward the lines I saw another Fokker biplane badly crashed on the ground just east of Armentières in a trench."

When the British ground offensive at Amiens began, the 17th Aero Squadron was ordered to escort 211 RAF Squadron on a series of raids on the docks at Bruges. It was dangerous work requiring the aircraft "to fly out to sea and attack from east of the target, this making it a very long trip over the lines."[35] On one raid two Fokkers appeared out of the sun and Ralph Gracie was falling earthwards in flames before he'd barely had time to react. Two more pilots were wounded, including Ralph Snoke, another of the eight original members of 17th Aero Squadron.

Colonel Jack Cunningham, C.O. of the 65th Wing, wanted a "show," something spectacular with which to delight the RAF top brass. Studying the map of the Flanders sector, he pointed to a large German airfield at Varsenare, a few miles to the west of Bruges. It was home to at least five squadrons of Gothas and Fokkers, all of whom were responsible for considerable inconvenience in recent days, and Cunningham had received word that the château on the northeast corner of the field was the pilots' quarters. He wanted it bombed.

There was a problem, however: the target lay thirty miles behind German lines. Scrupulous planning would therefore be required

---

[35] Frederick Mortimer Clapp, *A History of the 17th Aero Squadron*

by the four fighter squadrons chosen to support 211 Squadron for the raid: 17th and 148th, and 210 and 213 Squadrons RAF. Cunningham organized a series of dummy raids in the Calais area, "with the approach and departure in predetermined formations to avoid collisions." He even took to the air in a Camel, accompanied by Sam Eckert and Harold Fowler, to supervise the dress rehearsals.

On August 11, two days before the raid, 148th Aero Squadron was moved out of the 65th Wing, and transferred south to reinforce the RAF in the Amiens sector. Their sister squadron, 17th Aero, saw them off in fine style, hosting an extravagant dinner in the mess on the night of August 12, what Clapp later described as a "great evening."

August 13 dawned misty as Hamilton and Goodnow led their men toward the machines being run up by their ground crew. Among the twelve pilots chosen

Colonel Jack Cunningham, commanding officer of the 65th Wing, was an aggressive leader.

for the mission were Frank Dixon, Merton Campbell, Robert Todd, and William Shearman. Initially everything went according to plan. The four squadrons rendezvoused over the sea, each machine carrying four Cooper bombs, with the exception of flight commanders who had phosphorous bombs to drop near the machine gun emplacements guarding the aerodrome.

The flock of aircraft flew up the coast at 2,500 feet, clouds whipping across the aircraft and scattering the formation. Lieutenant Colonel Cunningham became separated from the rest of the raiders, as did Dixon.

Looking down from his cockpit, Hamilton recognized the port of Zeebrugge up ahead. He banked to the right and went into a shallow dive, with the other ten Camels of 17th Aero squadron following in perfect formation as the target came into view. An RAF communique described what happened:

> After the first two Squadrons had dropped their bombs from a low height, machines of No. 17th American Squadron dived to within 200

feet of the ground and released their bombs, then proceeded to shoot at hangars and huts on the aerodrome, and a chateau on the N.E. corner of the aerodrome was also attacked with machine gun fire. The following damage was observed to be caused by this combined operation: a dump of petrol and oil was set on fire, which appeared to set fire to an ammunition dump; six Fokker biplanes were set on fire on the ground, and two destroyed by direct hits from bombs; one large Gotha hangar was set on fire and another half demolished; a living hut was set on fire and several hangars were seen to be smoldering as the result of phosphorus bombs having fallen on them. In spite of most of the machines taking part being hit at one time or another, all returned safely, favorable ground targets being attacked on the way home.

Colonel Cunningham had been the first to return to Petite Synthe, followed a short while later by Dixon, who having lost contact with the squadron, went off on a lone bombing mission to Ostend. The pair stood by their machines, surrounded by ground crews, peering at the oyster gray sky to their east. "One by one the pilots came back, their machines badly shot up, but they themselves safe and sound," remembered Clapp. Each of the American pilots was accorded a hero's return as he leapt down from his machine. Questions came thick and fast and the answers in excited, breathless tones. Hamilton described how he'd "dropped four bombs on north hangars from 200 feet, shot fifty rounds into the windows of the château, made four circuits of the field shooting at a row of five Fokkers on the ground with engines running." Todd explained that his four bombs had landed on the château, from no more than 250 feet. Did he see any other damage? "Saw seven enemy machines burning on the ground."

Lieutenant Albert Schneider had seen a pilot climb into the cockpit of his Fokker. He admired his courage, but he still opened fire and shot the man dead. Shearman couldn't say the damage caused by his bombs but he'd killed one man running toward a machine gun emplacement, fired a long burst into four Fokkers on the ground, and "on my way home [fired] at the crew of the anti-aircraft gun to the west of the aerodrome."[36]

[36] At the end of the war, a German report on the raid revealed that fourteen of their aircraft had been destroyed in the raid and "over one hundred and twenty soldier mechanics and about thirty pilots killed."

Cunningham had done it; he had pulled off a "show" that soon brought a warm message of congratulation from the Chief of the American Air Service. Addressed to Maj. Harold Fowler, the letter ran:

> This office is in receipt of your letter of August 16th enclosing the details of the work of the 17th Aero Squadron on August 13th in its attack of the German airdrome at Varssenaere [sic]. Chief of Air Service is particularly pleased with the splendid work done by this squadron on the date mentioned. It shows the aggressiveness and working together as a squadron, which we are endeavoring to obtain for all units of the American Air Service.
>
> I have furnished a copy of your report to the Intelligence Section, General Staff, who have informed me that they were greatly pleased with the work done and have cabled the information back to the United States for publication.
>
> Please express to the Squadron Commander, pilots and soldiers of the Squadron the appreciation of the Chief Air Service for the excellent work performed by them.
>
> [Signed] R. O. Van Horn, Colonel, A.S., Assistant, C.A.S.

Lloyd Hamilton was awarded the British Distinguished Flying Cross (DFC) for his "dash and skill" during the raid on Varsenare. Other members of 17th Aero squadron involved in the attack were less fortunate. Within twenty-four hours, two were dead. William Shearman was shot down and killed on an offensive patrol, and, a couple of hours later, Lyman Case's tail was sliced off by an enemy aircraft out of control at 14,000 feet. The German pilot had been shot dead by Glenn Wicks, a horrified witness as his friend's machine "went straight down flopping about."

Wicks was killed later in the summer, as was Merton Campbell, shot down on August 23. Five days before the death of Campbell, 17th Aero Squadron had moved south to Auxi-le-Château, where the previous month the top British ace, James McCudden, had been killed in a flying accident. Death seemed to claim them all in the end, even the very best.

Hamilton was some way short of McCudden's fifty-seven victories when he arrived at Auxi-le-Château, but he was proving to be one of the top American aces that summer. On August 20, Hamilton wrote his parents in Vermont that he hoped his new base would prove a "happy hunting ground." It did. The following day he took his tally

Unlike British pilots, balloon observers were issued parachutes; this one has just been deployed.

to nine, shooting down a Fokker and then an observation balloon. August 21 also marked the opening day of the Battle of Bapaume, an offensive launched by the British Third Army, and the second phase of the Battle of Amiens.

Campbell was killed in a low-level bombing sortie, and by August 24, the strain was beginning to tell on the squadron. Wicks described it in a letter home as "strenuous and nervous work to say the least." Even Hamilton felt a sense of foreboding, telling the squadron's medical officer, Lt. Jacob Ross, an old friend from the University of Syracuse, that "if this push continues, you will be writing home to my parents."

Shortly after midday on Saturday August 24, Hamilton took off, accompanied by Lt. Jesse Campbell. The pair turned northeast toward the German lines. This was to be a day of improvisation, attacking targets as and when they arose. At 2:10 p.m. they bombed an enemy building close to the Bapaume to Cambrai road, and then they headed north to an observation balloon they could see. "We attacked an enemy balloon at about 1,000 feet," wrote Campbell in his report. "I fired 150 rounds at close range and [the] balloon burst into flames and went down. I saw Lieut. Hamilton firing all the way down at close range on it."

Suddenly Hamilton's Camel shuddered, and then went into a spin. Campbell was forced to climb away from the scene because of intense ground fire. Back at Auxi-le-Château, he told Dr. Ross that Hamilton had been hit but he hadn't seen his fate thereafter. That evening Ross wrote to Hamilton's parents. He recounted Campbell's description of the incident but was straight with them. There was a good chance their son was dead, he wrote, but they should cling to "the small hope that 'Ham' might still be alive and a prisoner."

As Ross wrote Hamilton's parents, the missing pilot's best friend, William Tipton, sat slumped in the mess, alone with his grief. The whole of the next day, recalled Frederick Clapp, Tipton "played the gramophone to himself, holding his big, slightly bald, blond head in his hands, a dead cigar in the corner of his mouth. He did nothing but stare into the gramophone, while it wheezed and growled and squeaked out 'Old Bill Bailey,' 'The Mississippi Volunteers,' or 'Poor Butterfly.'"

On August 26, the 17th Squadron was instructed to assist the 148th Aero Squadron providing escorts to low-level bombing missions. Tipton led off eleven Camels, climbing slowly into a howling gale with winds up to 70 miles per hour. "Crossing the lines there were several Fokkers which attacked us, with several other flights of Fokkers coming through the clouds on us," recalled Frank Dixon. "I was not very high. In the general mêlée one

William Tipton of 17th Squadron survived being shot down to spend the rest of the war a prisoner.

Fokker appeared in front of me. I fired, he went over in his back and down."

Dixon spotted another Fokker closing in on a Camel. He intercepted the enemy aircraft and sent it into the ground with a short twenty-round burst. "Then my only thought was to get home," he admitted. "Believe me, at such a low altitude, with pom-poms following me at every quick maneuver, it was no cinch. I managed to arrive back at the squadron. . . . Tipton, Todd, Frost, Jackson, Bittinger, and Roberts did not."

In time, word was received that Howard Bittinger, Lawrence Roberts, and Harry Jackson—the latter on his first offensive mission—were dead. A month later, a postcard arrived at the squadron through the Aviation Officer in London. It was from Tipton. He, Todd, and Frost were all prisoners of war.

CHAPTER 16

Nerves Worn to a Frazzle

While the 17th Aero Squadron was being assembled at Petite Synthe, poor Orville Ralston had been reduced to a ferry pilot, transporting aircraft across the Channel to France so that some young daredevil could fly them into combat. He wondered what he'd done wrong. The answer was nothing. But despite his skills as a pilot, "Tubby" wasn't like Springs, Hamilton, or Callender; he didn't have a face that people remembered or a personality that attracted attention. His file sat buried on a desk somewhere, gathering dust, while he gathered planes and flew them to the front.

It was the same role assigned Arthur Taber; he, however, reveled in the job. Throughout the summer of 1918 he kept his parents abreast of his travels: a few days down to Bordeaux, a trip here and there to the seaside ("the smooth, hard sand-beach made an ideal place for landing"), up to Scotland, down to Cambridge, and then a few days in London. "I'm overworked," he complained to his mother. "All I do is fly, fly, fly new planes." What he wanted, he added, what was his most fervent desire, was a posting to a fighter squadron. "The men in our squadrons at the front have been having a gorgeous time firing up the retreating Hun while flying one hundred feet up only, and I wish more than words can say that I'd been with them."

Orville Ralston flew the DH.4 bomber before joining 85 Squadron.

On July 6, Ralston took matters into his own hands. In France on another ferrying mission he paid a courtesy call to 85 Squadron at St. Omer. Elliott Springs was no longer with them, but Larry Callahan was still there. Perhaps it was he who introduced his compatriot to Maj. Mick Mannock, recently arrived to replace Billy Bishop.

Mannock was a brilliant pilot, with fifty-two kills to his name, but he should never have been at the front. He was sick, physically and mentally, convinced that he had a rendezvous with death. His attitude certainly made him even more savage in the air. He hated Germans, and, starting July 7, he shot down nine in nineteen days.

Mannock was a thirty-one-year-old Anglo-Irishman, a shy, socially diffident man who felt an outsider because he lacked the privileged swagger of so many young British pilots. Perhaps in Ralston he recognized a kindred spirit. He accepted him into the squadron, and even made him 85's bartender, the position vacated by Springs.

Ralston couldn't have wished for a better mentor than Mannock. He was a theorist, a pilot who weighed up each risk and never dived recklessly into attack. Much of what he taught Ralston the American already knew, about the best angle of attack and every instructor's favorite phrase—"beware the Hun in the Sun." But Mannock passed on to Ralston some of his own combat rules: keep yourself physically fit; look after your guns as if they're your children; enemy fighters should be attacked from above, but two-seaters from under their tail; open fire when you're within one hundred yards of the target; aim for the pilot and keep firing until you've hit him. His philosophy of dogfighting was a metaphor for his life—don't get involved, stay on the periphery, and look for a clear target. Then attack swiftly and withdraw from the scrap.

If Mannock said he wanted Ralston in his squadron, then have him he would. No administrative officer could stand in the way of Britain's most ruthless ace. The young Nebraskan was soon filling his diary with ribald accounts of life in the RAF's most glam-

The great British ace Mick Mannock replaced Billy Bishop as C.O. of 85 squadron and took Orville Ralston under his wing, in time turning the young Nebraskan into an ace.

orous fighter squadron. One memorable night in the mess involved Callahan on the piano leading the squadron in an evening of ragtime. "Two great kegs of beer were near at hand and everyone was 'quaffing' beer," wrote Ralston. "Late in the evening we sat around the anteroom smoking, singing and I finally got out my old uke. Whiskey toddies were frequent and we sang and played around with Major Mannock as happy and boyish as the worst of us."

On July 24, Ralston scored his first victory when his flight came upon six Fokker D.VIIs northwest of Armentières. Remembering Mannock's advice, he singled out one of the six and attacked from above. "He turns slightly and goes into a vertical dive," Ralston wrote in his diary. "I follow at a terrible rate and fire my remaining shots from the Lewis drum. He still dives on. The speed is so terrific that I flatten out at 5,000 [feet] and see the Hun go on down and vertically into the ground."

Ralston returned to base, intoxicated by his success. Like Springs, Grider, Callahan, and every fighter pilot, the first victory tasted the best. "Believe me, it was great sport," he wrote in his diary that night. "I was thoroughly crazed over the fight."

Like so many aces, Britain's James McCudden was killed in the last few months of the war.

His euphoria was short-lived. Two days later Mannock crashed in flames, shot down by ground fire in a moment of carelessness after dispatching another Hun. Hadn't he told Ralston never to come down low to inspect the wreckage of your kills? In Mannock's honor, 85 Squadron threw an almighty wake with "music, liquor and a 'hilarious' time." Ralston found it hard to join in. "I guess there is no doubt it will come to all of us in the end," he wrote in his diary.

Ralston shot down his second German on August 22. A fortnight later he received orders transferring him to 148th Aero squadron. He was furious. It was all Elliott Springs's doing, aided—albeit unwittingly—by his old friend from 85 Squadron, Capt. Malcolm McGregor, who in passing had mentioned to Springs the sharp-eyed Nebraskan in his flight.

Springs was on the lookout for good pilots, so he arranged for Ralston's transfer. That wasn't all, he told his father in a letter dated September 10. "I have at last succeeded in getting Larry Callahan in my flight. He arrived yesterday."

Springs was overjoyed to welcome Callahan to the 148th. Although he had only accrued a modest tally of three enemy aircraft since arriving in France in May, Callahan was an emotional crutch for the increasingly worn Springs. Since August 8, the first day of the Battle of Amiens, Springs had been on countless low-level offensive patrols over enemy lines. That was pressure enough, but the responsibility of command weighed heavily on his young shoulders. In England, Springs had cultivated an image of insouciance—the happy warrior who lived only for women, wine, and war—but the reality was different. Conscientious, and deeply concerned for the welfare of the men in his flight, he wrote his mother on August 8 that "the excitement and strain is trebled for the leader. . . . [W]hen you are responsible for all that takes place from the time you leave the ground you find the old frazzle on the nerves."

Unwilling to confide in his father, Springs instead revealed some of his anxieties to his stepmother, a woman with whom he had only a lukewarm relationship. "I fought Huns all night in my sleep," he told her on August 14, a day after he'd claimed his sixth victory. "Today I feel all washed out." Three days later, after a ferocious dogfight between eleven Sopwith Camels and twenty Fokkers, Springs wrote he was unsure what would get him first, "a bullet or nervous strain." But to his comrades he maintained the pretense of nonchalance, using for his flight commanders' streamers a pair of ladies' silk stockings.

Then came the joint escort operation with 17th Aero Squadron on August 26, a murderous day that left three of the 17th dead and three more in captivity. It was, Springs wrote home, "the hardest scrap of my career." He came through unscathed but it had left him "feeling really depressed." What he needed was the company of Callahan, he told his mother, explaining that he was trying to prize him from 85 Squadron. "If so it ought to help a lot as my nerves are worn to frazzle."

Springs brightened the moment he saw Callahan saunter through the mess, kit bag slung over his shoulder, as imperturbable and inimitable as ever. Callahan had just returned from two weeks' leave in London, and within minutes Springs was laughing so much his sides ached. Callahan had passed part of the time as a guest of Col. Bishop, now head of the Canadian Flying Corps, and the rest of the leave was shamelessly spent in the most disreputable clubs of the British capital. "Every blonde and brunette is weeping for Grider," reported Callahan. Well, almost. Billie Carleton "has recovered sufficiently to become engaged to another American officer."[37]

The remaining two Musketeers vowed to make up for lost time. On September 11, the pair went to dine in a village bistro some ten miles from their new base at Remaisnil, where they had been moved to support the British Third Army in the Battle of Bapaume. It was an intimate dining room, crowded with "British colonels, a couple of stray Australian and Canadian majors and a sprinkling of Scotch and French dining there also." But what a flat atmosphere! Springs looked at Callahan. Without a word his friend rose and took his seat behind the piano in the corner of the room. "Almost immediately everyone became bosom friends," explained Springs to his mother. "A couple of the English officers were so affected by Larry's rag [time] that they gave an excellent imitation of the Gaity chorus and put on a very good

[37] Billie Carleton died of a drug overdose on November 28, 1918, the day after celebrating the end of the war at the Victory Ball in London's Albert Hall. The subsequent inquest, full of salacious accounts of the actress's drug habit and sexual promiscuity, gripped Britain and led to the tightening of anti-drugs legislation.

ballet. We all parted friends and we're going over some night to dine with a couple of the English officers at their mess."

The next evening, September 12, Callahan and Springs dropped in at 148th Aero Squadron to celebrate with George Vaughn, their old friend from the *Carmania*. After a slow start with 84 Squadron, Vaughn had embarked on a devastating killing spree, resulting in the award of the DFC. "In all," concluded the medal's citation, "he has accounted for six enemy aircraft, five machines destroyed and one driven down completely out of control, and one kite balloon." Vaughn had subsequently been transferred to the 17th to fill the empty chairs left in the mess by the disastrous events of August 26.

Although Orville Ralston had shot down two enemy aircraft, he'd been flying an S.E.5. Now he had to master the inferior Sopwith Camel. Ralston didn't appreciate its lack of agility but it was the machine's rotary engine that caused him the greatest anxiety. "I really am afraid I cannot fly them," he wrote in his diary on September 10. Disclosing his fears to Morton Newhall, 148th's commander, Ralston was given a

Known as the Arizona Balloon-Buster, Frank Luke of 91st Squadron shot down eighteen enemy balloons before his death in September 1918.

choice: make good in a Camel, or spend the rest of the war in a low-level bombing squadron.

"The petrol and oil fumes [from the engine] make me very sick," he complained to his diary, adding that he had made a "bum landing" first time around. But he was not going to give in. "I want to try and make good here for all the fellows are real boys. . . . I only hope I will feel better and can learn to fly this soon without any accidents."

Springs and Callahan came to Ralston's rescue, the former giving him some intensive instruction, while Callahan and the young Nebraskan went for a walk. "We have a good talk over things in general and I decide to fly them and stick it out at all hazards," Ralston wrote in his diary of the man-to-man parley with Callahan.

Imbued with the faith of the Two Musketeers Ralston had soon mastered his Camel. On September 15, he and Springs pounced on an enemy two-seater, both taking a share of the credit in destroying the Halberstadt.

By now the Allied ground offensive was gaining momentum and the Germans were falling back east. On September 20, 148th Aero squadron moved twenty miles southeast from Remaisnil to Baizieux. Four days later, Springs led Ralston, Callahan, and the rest of C Flight on an early morning offensive patrol over the enemy line together with A and B Flights, commanded by Henry Clay and Field Kindley. They encountered a large patrol of Germans flying at 12,000 feet, the "pilots exceptionally good," as Springs wrote in his combat report. At first the odds were even, fifteen versus fifteen, but "more Fokkers kept coming up."[38]

Springs managed to shoot down one Fokker for his fifteenth victory, but "three E.A.s got hits on my plane." The Germans' incendiary bullets scorched his propeller, pierced two of his spars and came so close to the cockpit Springs "could smell the phosphorous."

Springs escaped, but, on returning to base, discovered "nineteen holes in my machine." One by one the rest of the squadron returned, all except Callahan. Someone had seen him go down in a spin. Springs paced up and down outside the mess, willing his friend to return. Then at midday the phone rang. It wasn't Callahan, but it was news of him. One of his spars had been shot out in the dogfight, causing

---

[38] A British A.A. battery crew later told 148th Aero they had counted fifty-three Fokkers in the ten-minute dogfight.

Lieutenant John Todd was a Scottish ace whose eighteen victories in 1918 were all achieved in a Sopwith Camel.

his right wing to buckle. He'd gone into a spin but managed to pull out and side slipped back over the line before crashing in no man's land upside down. How bad were his injuries, Springs enquired. No injuries. He was having a spot of lunch and would be back with the squadron in time for dinner.

On September 26, it was Orville Ralston's turn to experience that heady concoction of thrill and fear. Forced to leave the formation because of a defective engine, Ralston was heading back to base when he spotted five Fokkers driving down three Camels. He evened up the odds by latching on to the tail of an enemy aircraft, firing a burst, but then could only curse silently as his target fled into a thick cloud. He hesitated. Ralston knew that the unwritten rules of aerial combat stated pilots should never follow their enemy into the clouds because of the risk of collision. "However," wrote Ralston in his diary. "I knew old 'Mick', Major Mannock, used to do it so I thought I would try." He plunged into the cloud, heart thumping loud beneath the roar of his rotary engine, then emerged on the other side. He saw his prey but "there were also four Fokkers not far off, coming in my direction." Ralston fired a long burst into the lone Fokker, sending him spiraling to earth, and then turned back into the cloud just as the quartet of Fokkers opened up.

In the company of his ground crew and Springs, Ralston examined his engine upon his return. A cylinder was cracked so there had been no compression. Springs whistled appreciatively, and told Ralston he was some pilot to have weighed into a fight with a bad engine. Later he submitted a recommendation that Ralston be awarded the DSC for his "act of unusual daring and courage."

The next day Springs, together with Henry Clay, spotted five enemy aircraft approaching Allied lines near Cambrai. The pair "although hopelessly outnumbered, immediately attacked" and between them sent five hundred rounds into a two-seater. Then they fled home, Springs laughing that none of the Germans had managed to put a single bullet through his machine.

A short while later Springs suffered a breakdown. He couldn't remember the exact date; it was either the end of September or the beginning of October. He was transported to Paris and for several days lay in a hospital bed a "total nervous wreck." On October 8, he felt strong enough to write home, but he no longer cared about concealing the truth from his father. "I'm a chattering idiot they tell me and I'm expecting my hair to turn gray daily."

Major Leslie MacDill, the officer who had been in command of the Italian detachment a year earlier, had visited Springs and was trying to arrange a posting for him as an instructor to the U.S. aerial gunnery school at St. Jean de Monts on the west coast of France. Springs, however, recently promoted to major and now the recipient of both the DFC and DSC, was adamant he would return to lead his flight into battle once more.

However, the doctors laughed at Springs's suggestion he was fit enough to return to the front. Absolutely no way. Springs resigned himself to his plight. Anyway, there were worse places to be than the Hotel Continental, the plush establishment in 3 Rue de Castiglione that had been converted into a military hospital. His days were spent in "pleasant and philosophic contemplation of life in general." His spirits were buoyed by the news that "three of the men I lost have been reported as prisoners," and he was delighted that his old friend Bill Tipton was safe and well if also in German hands. "If only Mac [Grider] would show up," he wrote to his stepmother. "But that's beyond the realms of possibility now."

CHAPTER 17

Killed Doing
Noble Duty

Alvin Callender had returned to 32 Squadron in early September and to a new appointment as flight commander in place of the much mourned Jerry Flynn.[39]

As he prepared to return, Callender wrote his parents to explain that, much as he'd enjoyed his leave, he was eager to get back in the cockpit and "do a little execution" after "two weeks of loafing around on this side of the Channel."

The Western Front had altered radically in the two weeks Callender had been "loafing" in Britain. The Amiens offensive, launched on August 8, had been followed thirteen days later by the British Third Army's attack at Bapume. The German Second Army was in a headlong retreat toward the Hindenburg Line, falling back over a thirty-four mile front. On August 26, the British First Army joined the offensive, and three days later Bapaume fell. Then the Australian Corps were sent into battle, crossing the River Somme on August 31, and smashing through the German lines at St. Quentin Canal in a battle also involving British and American troops. On September 2, the Canadian Corps surged toward the Drocourt-Queant line, and, after a bloody engagement, ousted the Germans

---

[39] On the morning of September 12, Flynn's mother received two items of mail at her home in Waterloo, Ontario. One was a cheery letter from her son, dated August 13; the other a telegram from the Secretary of War reporting him missing.

from the psychologically important position. Now the Allies had control of the western edge of the Hindenburg Line, from where the previous March the Germans had launched their own great offensive.

The Hindenburg Line, constructed during the winter of 1916–1917 and named after the Prussian field marshal who had won a series of great victories on the Eastern Front in the first two years of the war, stretched approximately eighty miles from Arras in the north to the Aisne in the south. It was a defensive fortification built in anticipation of a great Anglo-French attack, designed to minimize German losses while allowing them to inflict huge casualties on the enemy. While containing their enemy on the western front, the Germans planned to force the British to the negotiating table. Air raids would be increased, as would submarine attacks on merchant shipping, so that the starving and demoralized British would have no alternative than to seek an end to the war.

However, the policy had failed, and now the German soldiers dug in on the Hindenburg Line in September 1918 were the ones demoralized, part of an army that had spent the last month retreating over ground it had fought so hard to capture the previous spring. One great big battle was clearly still to come: the all-out Allied attack on the Hindenburg Line. All the momentum was with their enemy, bolstered by thousands of fresh American soldiers, who were well equipped, well fed, and well motivated—a stark contrast to what remained of the once-great German army.

American Doughboys marching to war in October 1918 near the Argonne in France. *Library of Congress*

As the Allies gathered themselves for that final assault, the RAF Ninth Brigade was ordered to secure control of the air over the strategically important towns of Douai and Cambrai, and as far south as Saint-Quentin. Ninth Brigade comprised thirteen bomber and fighter squadrons, one of which was 32, and their role was to bomb targets and destroy as many enemy fighters as possible. Resistance was fierce, however; the German air force was aware that should the Hindenburg Line break, beyond lay open country and a clear route into Germany.

Frank Hale wrote his parents relating some of these developments on the evening of September 2. Apologizing for not having written for several days, he continued: "For the last three or four days I haven't had time to wash properly. We work from morning to night. . . . [O]ur front is constantly moving eastward."

On September 4 Hale shot down two Fokker D.VIIs, one north of Cambrai, the second a few minutes later southeast of Arras. Two days later, Bogart Rogers performed a similar feat, claiming two victories in the space of a few hours. For Rogers there was a sense of palpable relief to finally be back on the scoreboard six weeks after shooting down his first enemy aircraft. He told his fiancée about the first kill in a letter written the same day. It had been "darn fun," he exclaimed, swooping on a "a nice Hun two seater, fat, slow and comfortable," the crew too preoccupied taking reconnaissance photographs to spot him lurking at 20,000 feet.

On September 8, Hale threw a party in the squadron mess for some of his old buddies from the 4th Ambulance Company of Syracuse. As he told Rogers, Hale had last seen them on the Mexican border in 1916, but he'd heard they were in France, so the least he could do was show them a good time. "They were a fine lot of fellows, some of the best I've met out here," wrote Rogers. "These poor people in the infantry don't get an awful lot of joy out of life . . . [so] without throwing any sweet scented bouquets we can fix up a very attractive looking dinner. One of these fellows said it was the most beautiful sight he'd seen in France."

Hale spent the morning of September 16 visiting Lt. Donald Armstrong, one of his friends from Fayetteville serving in the 4th Ambulance Company. He returned to 32 Squadron for lunch, then in the afternoon composed a letter to his parents, telling them about Don and also about the toll being exacted by the constant flying. "I never thought that it would [be] such a nervous strain," he admitted. "The minute we cross the lines old Archie starts bursting all around. That is quite nerve-wracking. Also, a fellow is on edge every minute, looking around and attending to the dozens of different things necessary to see to. First you have to see that you keep the correct position in the formation. Then you are constantly on the alert for Hun machines. Also you have to watch all your instruments to see that your engine is getting the correct amount of oil, etc."

Hale included a couple of casual anecdotes and then brought the letter to a close. "Our inevitable afternoon tea is ready now," he wrote. "So I guess I'll close and go and be English for a few minutes." Unfortunately they wouldn't have much time to savor their tea, he noted, just half an hour in fact, and then "we have to go on an offensive patrol. That means going over the lines looking for a scrap."

One can imagine Hale's emotions as he replaced the cap on his fountain pen, slipped the letter inside an envelope, and asked an orderly to ensure it got mailed. Then he joined his comrades for tea, served on the squadron's best crockery, sinking into a comfortable armchair, sharing weak jokes, and emitting counterfeit bluster over cake, scones, and strawberry jam. It was the same in every mess in every squadron in every air force, men reaching deep into their soul to dredge up the last reserves of their willpower. Elliott Springs recalled a convivial evening in the 148th Aero's mess shattered by the shrill ring of the phone. It was headquarters. Instructions for a dawn patrol. "After they got the orders not a pilot could lift a glass to his mouth with one hand," wrote Springs.

The "scrap" Hale envisaged in the letter to his parents materialized. He and Rogers, both members of Callender's C Flight, engaged a flight of Fokkers over Cambrai a little after 6:00 p.m. "The place was simply cluttered up with airplanes," Rogers wrote home that evening. "Every time you turned you nearly bumped into one."

Rogers stayed calm, singling out a Fokker D.VII and pumping one hundred rounds into his tail. The machine went down in a spin and crashed in Sancourt, the same village a couple miles north of Cambrai where Callender's sixth victory fell to earth. Hale had to chase his Fokker a few miles north but close to the village of Brunemont the pursuit ended with the German falling in flames.

The Allies relaunched their offensive in the last week of September, determined to bring the war to an end by Christmas. On September 23, the Allied commander in chief, Marshal Foch, had accepted

Field-Marshal Haig's view for "concerted convergent action," and plans for four separate offensives were drawn up. There was little time between planning and execution. On September 26, the American First Army and French Fourth Army attacked between the Meuse and Reims, followed the next day by the British Third Army and the right of the British First Army advancing in the Cambrai sector. On September 28, the British Second Army, the Belgian Army, and nine divisions of the French Army would go on the offensive in Flanders, and the British Fourth Army and French First Army would assault the Hindenburg Line behind the St. Quentin Canal on September 29.

Nowhere were the gains as spectacular as those made by the British Third and First armies on September 27 as they advanced across the northern extension of the Hindenburg Line towards Cambrai, exploiting the success of the Canadian Corps at the start of the month at Drocourt-Queant. Canadian assault troops, supported by tanks, crossed the Canal du Nord and in two days an advance of six miles had been achieved on a twelve mile front. More than ten thousand Germans had surrendered, and the Allies expected far more as the Fourth Army prepared to launch the main attack on the Hindenburg Line.

It began in rain at 5:50 a.m., and the day was as bloody as expected. Poor visibility hampered the two inexperienced American divisions as they attacked the St. Quentin Canal, while supporting Australian units met fierce resistance on the high ground. Further south German defenses were less defiant, and Allied troops crossed the canal and captured a number of bridges intact. More brigades rushed up in support, and by mid-afternoon the main German positions along the Hindenburg Line had been breached, their soldiers either fleeing or surrendering.

"We have been having rather a lively time of it of late," wrote Alvin Callender to his sister on September 29. That was some understatement. No. 32 Squadron had been in continuous action for the past few days, fighting "very large German formations of from 20 to 40 aircraft." On September 24, Callender's C Flight, together with A and B Flights, took on twenty-four Fokkers attempting to attack a formation of British DH.9 bombers on their way back from a raid on Cambrai. Callender went for the German squadron commander, hitting him with his second burst, and watching the Fokker dive into the northern edge of Bourlon Wood. Three other E.A.s were shot down by 32 Squadron before Callender claimed his second victory of the day.

Offensive patrols continued for the next couple of days and then, on September 27, the day the big ground offensive began against Cambrai, 32 Squadron carried out one mission after another. In the morning they escorted a bombing raid on a German aerodrome and met fifteen Fokker D.VIIs from *Jasta* 5, their leader the great ace Fritz Rumey, who that month alone had shot down sixteen enemy aircraft to take his tally to forty-five.

Rumey was fearless—he had shot down more fighter aircraft (as opposed to two-seater aircraft) than Manfred von Richthofen—and he liked to single out enemy flight commanders. Spotting Callender's streamers, Rumey went for the American, but in his single-minded pursuit of his prey he overlooked Lt. Bruce Lawson, a South African, who "worked into position unobserved and fired both guns at point blank range." Rumey pulled up stalling but the top plane of his machine collided with Lawson's undercarriage. As the Fokker fell, Rumey undid his seatbelt, hauled himself out of the cockpit and jumped, putting his faith in his parachute. However, the 'chute failed to open, and Rumey plummeted to his death.

A Pfalz D.III decorated in the inimitable colors of *Jasta* 8.

Rogers meanwhile had shot down a Fokker, his fifth victory: cause for a celebratory lunch and a quick note to Isabelle. "It was a lovely target so I gave it to him with both guns," he wrote. "He slipped out, then burst into flames. It's a nasty sight, Izzy, even if it is a Hun."

A couple of hours later Rogers and the rest of 32 Squadron were back in the air on an offensive patrol. Hale was at 16,000 feet when he spotted ten Fokkers diving on a squadron of British bombers, "so like the brave man that I am not, I opened my throttle and went to their assistance."

The subsequent action was described by Hale in a letter to his parents dated September 30:

> I picked out one Hun and attacked him. I shot him down. His machine broke into bits in the air. Just then I heard the rat-tat-tat of a machine gun. I saw the tracer bullets flying by me.
>
> I instantly pulled my machine into a climbing turn. I did a half roll. That brought me down upon the fellow who just a minute before had been shooting at me. I held my fire until I nearly rammed him. Then I let him have a burst from both of my guns.
>
> He turned over a couple of times. Then he went down in flames. Again I heard machine guns in back of me [sic]. I guess all the eight remaining Huns were on my tail shooting at me.
>
> I knew it would be folly to try and fight the whole bunch. So down I went into a spin. I was headed for the clouds, which were 3,000 or 4,000 feet below me, and about that far from the ground. There was a strong west wind blowing, and I knew that I must have drifted back over the Hun lines for quite a distance.
>
> When I got down into the clouds I pulled out of the spin. I found myself going due east by compass. I didn't have any idea where I was by that time, so I pulled down under the clouds to see. As it happened I came out directly over Cambrai, which at that time was five or six miles back of the Hun lines. I immediately turned and started west again.
>
> Again I heard a machine gun. When I turned I saw a Hun below and behind me. Evidently he had followed me down, knowing I would have to come out of the clouds to get my bearings.
>
> I turned and dived at him with both guns firing. I missed him so I zoomed up, half-rolled, and dived at him again. This time I got him cold at point blank range. I let him have both guns. He went down like a brick. His ship burst into flames when it crashed.

Back at base, Hale submitted three combat reports, and within twenty-four hours confirmation was received by Maj. John Russell, 32's squadron commander, that wreckage of all three aircraft had been located. "The general heard about, and recommended me for a Distinguished Flying Cross," Hale told his parents. "Don't know whether I'll get it or not but can you imagine me going up to Buckingham Palace and having the king pin this medal on my breast?"

With the Hindenburg Line broken and the Allies advancing further east every day, everyone knew the war was nearing its end. Bulgaria signed an armistice with the Allies on September 30 and, on October 3, Kaiser Wilhelm II replaced Georg Hertling as Chancellor with Prince Maximilian of Baden, instructing the moderate nobleman to negotiate the most favorable armistice terms possible.

Even the weather over the Western Front appeared to have had enough after four years of bloodshed. A blanket of thick cloud moved in over northern France on the afternoon of October 2. Three days later it was still there, the rain as persistent as a German A.A. battery. Bogart Rogers went over to 92 RAF Squadron to look up an old friend from back home, Evandar Shapard from Tennessee. Alvin Callender went too. He needed a diversion. He hadn't been feeling well of late, confiding to an uncle in a letter the previous day that he needed a vacation: "Although I have nine to ten hours in bed every night I hardly sleep a wink. That is a common trouble among flying men."

Time dragged for much of October, the men hardly seeing a sniff of the enemy. Instead bridge, poker, and drinking were the order of the day, "also thick heads in the morning." On October 13, Callender wrote a friend that he heard the German people were ready to throw in the towel, adding: "Their air force opposite us already have practically."

Instead of dawn patrols, the men went off on early morning runs. There were table-tennis tournaments, and a soccer match that pitted A and B Flights against C Flight and Headquarters. A and B won by two goals to one. Rogers and Montague Tancock went grouse shooting with captured German rifles and angered the locals.

Callender's thoughts began turning to life after the war. "The main thing worrying me now is demobilization," he wrote a friend on October 30, three days after 32 Squadron had relocated to Pronville, west of Cambrai. "I expect we will find it a lot harder to get out of the army than it was to get in. It will take at least twelve months to get all of us Americans, Canadians and other Colonials home, and it will be my luck to get my ticket some time during the eleventh month, I expect. However, I won't mind that so much if I can joy ride around France and England in [an] airplane during that period."

Callender didn't have time to sign off his letter. Instead he was ordered to lead C Flight toward La Louvière and Manage as an escort for a squadron of British bombers. The weather had taken a turn for the better and, all along the front, squadrons were ordered into the air to bomb targets, photograph positions, and shoot down the last remnants of the German air force.

At 9:20 a.m., eight Fokker D.VIIs dove out of the sun on the bombers. Callender led his seven-strong flight to the rescue but suddenly another layer of Germans appeared. "There were Huns everywhere," recalled Rogers. "Above, below and on both sides." A and B Flights saw the danger but, by the time they arrived, C Flight had seen Lieutenants Farquhar, Wilderspin, and Amory spin out of the sky. "Every time you'd look around there would be more of them coming up," said Rogers. "I had two of 'em worry me almost to tears, one above and one below."

A fourth S.E.5a was hit and dropped from the fight, watched by soldiers of D Company, 116th (Ontario County) Canadian Infantry Battalion. The aircraft came to earth close to where the men were positioned just north of Valenciennes, and Lt. H. E. Patterson led his men to the wreckage.

The pilot had been shot through the lungs but Patterson detected a faint pulse. "We did all we could," Patterson wrote Alvin Callender's parents, but their son died an hour later without regaining consciousness. If it was any solace, added the Canadian, "he was killed doing noble duty."

October 30 was the high spot of the air war over the Western Front. Though the RAF had lost twenty-nine aircrew killed or missing, and a further eight wounded, the German air force had seen sixty-seven of their aircraft shot down. Such was the gallantry displayed by the RAF that King George V issued a Royal Tribute:

I offer you and the Royal Air Force my warmest congratulations on the successful results of air fighting on October 30, and on beating all previous records. Such achievements testify to the spirit which animates all ranks in their determination to maintain our mastery in the air and cannot fail materially to assist the steady advance of my Armies in the field.

George R.I., General-in-Chief

On November 2, 32 Squadron moved again, this time to La Brayelle airfield, an aerodrome close to Douai. It was a melancholic experience for Rogers. The squadron had only seven serviceable aircraft and nine pilots fit enough to fly. Two days later he wrote to his fiancée from their new quarters, an old French château, and apologized for the fact he hadn't written since October 30. "Fact is," he confessed. "I've never felt less like writing than I have the last few days." He told her about the "awful scrap" that has cost "poor old Callender" his life. He ended with another apology. "This isn't much of a letter, but the next ones will be better. I've had too much enthusiasm knocked out of me the last few days to be entertaining."

CHAPTER 18

Peace on the Horizon

George Vaughn's lethal streak that had begun with 84 Squadron in late July, and culminated a month later with the award of the DFC, continued in September with 17th Aero Squadron. On September 20, the squadron had moved from Petite Synthe to Soncamp, near Doullens, sharing the aerodrome with 87 RAF Squadron in readiness for the impending offensive at Cambrai against the Hindenburg Line.

Frederick Clapp, the 17th's adjutant, recalled that "we pitched our officers' tents and the two marquees that were to be the Mess in a triangle of pasture." Heavy rain and the tramp of flying boots churned the pasture into mud that was "omnipresent and deep." Two days after the move to Soncamp Vaughn shot down two enemy aircraft, a feat he dismissed in a sentence in a letter the following day. "Yesterday, by the way, I got two more Huns, which gives me a total of seven confirmed, I think."

Clapp later wrote a more florid account of the dogfight, recalling that "Vaughn saw fifteen Fokkers dive, as he thought, on our 'C' flight formation from 15,000 feet. Though outnumbered nearly five to one, he led his flight impetuously to the attack and, in the midst of furious and numerous 'bursts' fired by all our pilots, the results of which could not be observed because of the bewildering intensity of the engagement, he shot down one Fokker in flames and crashed another."

But the dead pilots' comrades were out for revenge. Vaughn recalled that seconds after shooting down the second Fokker, "a burst of bullets came through the three-ply over my knees. That sort of hurt my feelings and I stuck down my nose and twisted my machine into a spin. . . .

[T]hat spin out of the fracas seemed endless. My machine didn't give them a decent target, but two or three of those lads had made my acquaintance and yearned to know me better."

The two Germans on Vaughn's tail were Lt. Wilhelm Neuenhofen of *Jasta* 36 and Lt. Friederich Noltenius of *Jasta* 27, the latter of whom left an account of the dogfight. "Finally Neuenhofen got close enough, kept behind him and forced him down for good," wrote Noltenius. "I kept a bit higher up because the cloth covering of the top wing had torn off and several ribs were broken in the hectic dogfight. The kill was credited to Neuenhofen."

However, the two Germans had been presumptuous in imagining that their foe was dead. Vaughn had avoided a "long burst" fired by Neuenhofen, only to discover, as he shoved on the throttle, that he had no more gas. He looked for a place to land and "just as my wheels were about to rub the ground, I thought of my emergency tank. I had forgotten all about it."

Harold Shoemaker was one of 17th Squadron's aces, but his luck ran out in October 1918 when he was killed in a collision with fellow pilot Glen Wicks.

Vaughn turned on the petcock and punched the air with delight as gas flowed down to the carburetor and the motor roared its approval. "With one eye I negotiated the piles of barb wire and with the other I looked around for signs of tracer bullets. None were passing. The last square-nose was streaking it for home probably to turn in a report of the exact time and place of my crash."

Vaughn collected a DSC for this action, the citation mentioning how "he alone attacked an enemy advance plane which was supported by seven Fokkers and shot the advance plane down in flames."

When the great offensive began against the Hindenburg Line, 17th Aero carried out a series of bombing sorties, targeting transport and troop concentrations. There were high risk operations, wrote Vaughn, "and we were paying a heavy price for the low-level work." No day cost more that fall than October 6 when two of the squadron's most experienced, and popular pilots, Harold Shoemaker, an ace, and Glenn Wicks collided during a bombing "due to heavy and accurate anti-aircraft fire."

On October 14, Vaughn shot down two more enemy aircraft in a day, taking his tally to thirteen, and then was finally put out of action—by a "wisdom tooth so far back in my mouth that the gum had begun to grow over the top of it." He was carted off to hospital, operated on, and ordered to rest up for a week. When he returned to the squadron, he found everything in a state of flux. The 17th Aero Squadron had been ordered south, to Toul, in the American sector, where they would be equipped with French SPAD XIII fighters as part of the U.S. 4th Pursuit Group.

"We heard the news with mixed emotions," reminisced Frederick Clapp. "We wanted naturally to have some part in the exploits of our own people in the field. But we had been very happy with the British and had learned their game and how well they played it."

On October 30, the day before the squadron entrained south, Gen. Charles Longcroft, one of the RAF's senior commanders in France flew over in his Camel. The enlisted men were "drawn up on three sides of a hangar and he walked down their lines asking, here and there, one or another of them, what his work had been before the

Shoemaker, front row, far right, with some of his fellow pilots from 74 squadron shortly before his transfer to the 17th.

war and in the Squadron." Longcroft then removed from his tunic a letter and read it aloud to the officers and men stood before him. It was, he declared, from General Byng, commander of the Third British Army.

"Will you please convey to the Commanders and all ranks of the 17th and 148th American Squadrons my sincere appreciation of their excellent and valuable work with the Third Army, and thank them very warmly for so cordially responding to all the calls made upon them.

"I greatly regret their departure and wish them every luck."

CHAPTER 19

There I Lived a Life

Elliott Springs returned from his Paris hospital to the 148th Aero Squadron on October 29. They, too, had been ordered south to Toul, but amid all the upheaval of the move, Springs found the time to hear an account of the previous day's action from Larry Callahan. All three flights had gone out on an offensive patrol, in layers, with Callahan's B Flight (he had taken over command from Springs) on top, C in the middle, and A flying at the lowest altitude of 10,000 feet. Once inside enemy territory a flight of seven Fokkers was spotted away to the east. A trap was laid, A Flight the bait. It took a few minutes for the enemy to spring the trap; the German pilots also knew the war was practically over. They too were thinking ahead to the future, not wishing to take unnecessary risks at this late stage. Only when the German flight commander was confident it was no trap did the Fokkers attack. As they dove down on A Flight, the other two flights came down from above. None of the Germans escaped.

One of the seven was shot down by Callahan, his fifth victory. At last! he told Springs. An ace. He also received the DFC for his part in the ambush, the citation noting that his B Flight had accounted for all of the downed Fokkers. It added: "This officer has accounted for four EA crashed and one driven down out of control; he has proven himself an exceptionally fine patrol leader and has at all times displayed gallantry, initiative and devotion to duty of the highest order."

Callahan was delighted to welcome back Springs to the squadron but it was clear he wasn't the same man, the same Musketeer. He was tired, embittered, querulous, no longer the charming company he once had been. While Callahan, Ralston, and the rest of the 148th boarded a cattle train on November 1 for the journey to Toul, Springs rode in a Cadillac with the squadron commander, Mort Newhall, along with Henry Clay and Field Kindley.

They arrived at Toul to find the squadron "very fed up" and Springs was similarly exasperated when no news was forthcoming about his promotion to squadron commander. Major Fowler had promised him and Clay their own squadrons, and Springs had already inked in Callahan and Bim Oliver for flight commanders, but now everything was on hold. "Jesus Christ what a place! What an Army!" Springs seethed to his diary on November 7. "Chills and fever, am sick as a dog."

Springs spent the next day in bed with his fever. By November 9, he felt strong enough to write his stepmother, but it was more a diatribe than a letter. Every sentence bristled with hostility, against people back home, against the American military, against his father, against her. He told his stepmother to stop sending any more editions of the *Charlotte Observer*. "I'm infernally sick of reading in each issue where 'Mrs. Walter Lambeth and little daughter Mary Wisdom' are . . . and the location of Mrs. Gordon Finger's relatives." Didn't these people realize there was a war on? That over in Europe hundreds of American boys were dying each day?

As well as 17th and 148th Aero Squadrons, Toul was also home to the 25th Aero Squadron. They had arrived on October 24, minus any aircraft, and it wasn't until the first week of November that they began to take delivery of their S.E.5 fighters. Commanding the 25th was Reed Landis, one of the original fifty-two cadets who sailed to England in August 1917 aboard RMS *Aurania*. He had made quite a name for himself flying with 40 RAF Squadron, shooting down twelve enemy aircraft and earning the DFC and DSC. On August 8, he had accounted for two German machines and a kite balloon, characteristic of a man who "on all occasions engaged the enemy with marked skill and an entire disregard of personal danger."

Landis was anxious to get his squadron in the air before the armistice was signed. He, like everyone, knew it was imminent. On November 9, Germany proclaimed itself a republic and the Kaiser announced his abdication. If the 25th didn't carry out an offensive patrol before peace came, the squadron wouldn't qualify as an aerial

Observation balloons were not quite as easy a kill as many novice pilots imagined because of the numerous ground AA batteries nearby

pursuit unit operating on the front. On November 10, Landis led the 25th over the lines toward Metz in search of the enemy. No enemy aircraft were seen but the squadron was now active.

At 5:00 a.m. Paris time on November 11, an armistice was agreed between Germany and the Allied powers, to come into effect six hours later, at the eleventh hour of the eleventh day of the eleventh month. At 10:55 a.m. Landis set out on another patrol toward Metz, so he could say that the 25th were "operational" when the guns fell silent for the final time. He invited along three of his friends from the 148th: Orville Ralston, Bim Oliver, and Larry Callahan. "[We] take up the four new S.E.5s of 25 squadron and do a last war patrol," wrote Ralston in his diary. "We see nothing and have a line flip as the machines are wonderful and run fine. We 'high tone' the other squadrons down here by taking off in formation."

All four aircraft returned safely. Landis, Callahan, Ralston, and Oliver climbed out of their cockpits, shook each other's hands, and retired to the mess. The war was over; time for champagne.

Peace! Was it really true? Men wrestled with a welter of emotions. For Donald Poler, one of the original Warbirds, the armistice was a nuisance. He'd served with 40 RAF Squadron throughout the summer, shot down two balloons and an aircraft, and was now one of the 25th Aero Squadron's flight commanders. He felt "let down" by the end of the war. "I was ready to go still farther," he recalled. "Most of us were disappointed that the Armistice was signed. Most of us felt as though we hadn't done anything yet."

George Vaughn had done plenty. There was "quite a bit of rejoicing," he told his parents in a letter the next day, written with a slightly thick head. In the afternoon he and some of the boys of the 17th Aero Squadron took a ride into Toul. "I have never seen anything like the changed general atmosphere about the place," wrote Vaughn. "Everyone was wearing a broad 'won't come off' smile, and big ribbons or flags of their national colors. Flags were everywhere, in every conceivable place, and every motor car or truck carried large flags down the streets. In the square an American band was giving a concert, and a good one, too, assisted by someone who had evidently been a professional comedian in civil life."

Bogart Rogers didn't know how he felt now that the war had ended. There was soaring relief that he had come through unscathed. "I surely thank God it is [over] and that I'm here to see the finish," he wrote his fiancée, shortly after the Armistice had come into effect. But the silence unnerved him. No distance rumble of guns, no engine being run up on the aerodrome, no telephone ringing with fresh orders for a patrol. Just quiet. "Somehow or other it didn't seem possible it was all over," he wrote, "that we were thru with crossing the line and worrying about Huns and archie and seeing good fellows getting bumped off."

Good fellows like Alvin Callender. "Poor old Callender, as square and decent a man as ever lived," he told Isabelle, "going only a week or so ago." It wasn't fair. He cursed the war, and the politicians and everyone else who prattled on "about war being the salvation of nations, the one thing that can keep them from decay." It was a lie, declared Rogers. "I know that it will never be worth the sacrifice. It's all wrong."

Peace left Elliott Springs bereft. "No more can I laugh at conventions, colonels and cocktails, no more can I speak of shoes and ships and sealing wax with equal objectivity," he wrote. Soon he would have to return to civilian life, and its accompanying squalidness and pettiness, where money was considered by many—including his

Together with Landis, Bim Oliver, and Larry Callahan, Orville Ralston flew a final patrol with 148th Squadron at 10:55 on November 11, 1918.

The 94th, otherwise known as the Hat-in-the-Ring squadron, received greater recognition back in the United States because it was never under British control.

father—to be more important than integrity. "There is no longer that place where every man is known by his merit," he wrote mournfully, "where a grim though sure justice prevails, and where is always a haven of rest for those whom the world treats ill."

Springs followed Vaughn into Toul, watched the French dancing and the band playing, but he could "find no enthusiasm." He quailed at the future before him, bleak meaningless years, probably following his father into the cotton business. Springs thought of John McGavock Grider and all his other friends and comrades who had "gone west," and he knew that "no matter where I go or what I do, the best part of me will always remain between Zeebrugge and Armentières, and in front of Cambrai. There I lived a life, a long lifetime, there lie my companions, and many adversaries and there also lies the biggest part of myself."

Arthur Taber was at Ford Junction aerodrome in Sussex, England, when news came through of the Armistice. He wrote his mother an hour after peace descended across Europe, posing the question on the lips of most American service personnel. "When are we going home?" Soon, he hoped, and once back in the States he would ponder his future. The law? Business? Or perhaps remain in the military. "I'm convinced that aviation is 'here to stay'," Taber told his mother, "and its development will be lightning-like and colossal, and that it will continue to progress under government supervision; therefore it will be of advantage to be in the army, if one expects to continue to be associated with aviation."

The letter finished, Taber headed to London where for a few precious hours he surrendered to the unrestrained joy of the occasion. "It was an amazing sight to see London gone mad," he wrote his father a few days later. "People dancing in the street, parades everywhere, soldiers shooting off pistols, guns, etc., in the streets, a huge bonfire in Trafalgar Square of the captured Hun guns on exhibition in the Mall, a taxi-cab burning up in Piccadilly Circus, Roman candles and sky-rockets set off from the tops of busses and falling upon the human sea which thronged the streets beneath. . . . [T]he deliverance of these people from the four years' war-cloud is stirring to behold; I've never been so emotionally stirred."

People celebrate the news of Germany's surrender on Wall Street in November 1918.
Photograph by W. L. Drummond, courtesy Library of Congress

CHAPTER 20

Homecoming

A surprise arrived for 32 Squadron a couple of days after the Armistice—a visit from John Donaldson. The last anyone had seen of the young ace from North Dakota, he was spinning down to the ground on September 1. Now he was splashed all over the newspapers, describing how the Germans took him to a temporary prison camp in the village of Conde, where he shared a cell with another captured American pilot, Lt. Oscar Mandel. The pair jumped from a second floor window and made their way to the nearest German airfield, where they examined the aircraft and picked out a two-seater observation machine to fly back to their lines. "At dawn we got the plane in shape to fly," Donaldson told the papers. "Just then a German mechanic approached and discovered us. He raised hell. We grabbed him and in the tussle he stabbed me in the back. Mandel put him out of commission by hitting him over the head with a flashlight. Then we ran for it."

The two Americans were subsequently recaptured, but, on September 26, they were at it again, absconding from their new prison in the town of Valenciennes by cutting a hole in the roof of their cell with a piece of broken saw that they had stolen. Five men escaped in total but they soon decided to split up to improve their chances of making it to the Dutch border. On October 14, Donaldson and two of his companions, a pair of American pilots—Theose Tillinghast and Robert Anderson—reached the frontier between Belgium and Holland. "We spent a week reconnoitering to find a place to cross," explained Donaldson. "This was hard because there was an electric wire barrier charged with 3,000 volts. Finally we discovered an opening and crawled for fours on our bellies making all of 100 yards. Then we waited until the German sentries were far apart, stood up and ran like hell to Holland, which was half a mile away. We heard a yell and a shot but did not stop."[40]

Rogers told his fiancée he "never liked the chap personally and still don't," but it was a fine effort and Donaldson deserved the praise he was getting.

There was a crushing sense of anti-climax to life in the squadron post-war. Rogers felt no affinity to the new faces in the mess, the young pilots who had come out in the last weeks of the war. A chasm separated their experiences from his own. "Nearly half the flying officers haven't been over the line more than two or three times," he wrote home. "When you've been thru the mill with fellows, been in all sorts of tight places where you've helped them and they've helped you, there is a mutual feeling that isn't possible with fellows who've come out just about as the war ended."

Fred Libby and John Donaldson both received decorations from King George V. *Library of Congress*

On November 21, Rogers, Frank Hale, and another officer went in search of Alvin Callender's grave. They'd tried a week earlier, with no success, but this time they found it. The wreckage of his S.E.5 still lay on the ground, a few hundred yards from a cluster of houses. The three airmen sifted through the twisted fragments of metal with professional interest, theorizing about what must have happened. They were shocked by the number of bullet holes: "the machine had simply been shot to pieces," wrote Rogers.

A local farmer guided them to where Callender lay, close to his farmhouse. Rogers was upset that the grave was unmarked so "we put up the cross and then sodded the top and built a little border

[40] Tillinghast was nothing if not resilient. In 1933 he was one of seven survivors from a plane crash in Denver that killed five fellow passengers. He eventually rose to become president of the United Aircraft Service Corporation and died in 1982, aged eighty-eight. Anderson became a successful Hawaiian composer whose songs included "Lovely Hula Hands" and "Mele Kalikimaka."

of bricks around the edges." One of the officers took a photograph of Rogers beside the cross: something to send to Callender's family. They removed their caps, bowed their heads, and stood for a few moments in silence. "It was a solemn party that came home," he told his fiancée.

Rogers, recently promoted to captain, left France on leave on December 3, relieved to be rid of the graves and memories of friends, and glad also to be free of a squadron ravaged by influenza. In all, thirty members of thirty-two had been hospitalized on account of the pandemic sweeping the world, but only one man had died. Not so in England, Rogers wrote his girlfriend, where "there have been 32,000 deaths . . . in six weeks."

Rogers was back with the squadron just before Christmas. Still no definite news on when he might return to the States, and to her, he told his fiancée on December 26. They had received a lecture on demobilization and "things looks very encouraging." Fingers crossed repatriation would begin in early February.

New Year's Eve 1918 was a "quiet affair" at 32 Squadron. They were invited to a dance at another aerodrome, but most of the officers present were fresh out from England. There was no bond. Rogers and a few of the old hands returned to their mess, "made some rum punch, and sat in front of the fire until about four just talking."

Elliott Springs saw in the new year in Tours, central France, where the 2nd Aviation Instruction Center was based, at a ball attended by Gen. James G. Harbord, formerly General Pershing's chief of staff until, at the end of the war, he was assigned to take charge of troop and supply movement. There were plenty of junior officers in attendance, most fresh out from the States, the creases in their pants still razor sharp. They "bawl hell out of me on all occasions," wrote Springs in a letter to his stepmother on January 1. "I suppose I ought to feel lucky if these brave soldiers don't court-martial me."

Springs laughed at the Johnny-Come-Latelys. They could bawl as much as they liked. Usually they then pointed a dismissive finger at the small ribbon beneath his wings of diagonal stripes of white and deep purple and asked what it was.

"It's British," replied Springs more than once.

"Is it for service in a certain campaign?"

"No."

"Then it's for valor?"

Doug Campbell of the 94th Aero Squadron poses beside his French-made Nieuport 28.

"It's the DFC."

"Did you get it for getting a Hun?"

"No."

"What's it for, then?"

"They sometimes give it to people who get more than five."

Springs had finished the war with sixteen victories, and another decoration, the DSC, awarded for his "extraordinary heroism" of August 22 when he shot down three Fokker D.VIIs in the space of a few hours. Springs only learned of the award on December 31; by then he'd long since lost interest in the baubles of war. "They gave me a blank to full in," he told his stepmother. "Did I desire to remain in the regular army, reserve corps or get immediate and complete separation?" He chose the latter. "I'm coming home. I may be gray and tattered but I'm on my way."

He reckoned he'd be back in February. Until then he'd make the best of a bad job. Trips to Paris, and jaunts to Issoudun to see Larry Callahan and Bim Oliver, "who have been sitting around in the mud for six weeks."

George Vaughn had also been stuck in the mud of Issoudun for longer than he cared to remember. On November 25 he, Callahan, and Oliver—"three fellows who had been at the front the longest"—were ordered to the 3rd Aviation Instruction Center at Issoudun. Vaughn's hopes soared that he was on his way home. First in, first out. But no. "When we arrived here they told us we were to go through a very thorough physical examination to determine the effects of the war on the pilots who have survived it," he wrote his parents on November 28. "We spent the whole day yesterday in the hands of the 'Medical Research Board,' as they call it, and they are not through yet." It was a waste of time in his opinion, Vaughn told his parents. He was A-OK. "So I am afraid they have not learned much from their experiments on us."

Reunited and restless, Vaughn, Callahan, and Oliver sought distractions wherever possible at Issoudun. The center had a large Y.M.C.A. building and a Red Cross Hut, inside which air crew whiled away time, drinking and chatting and flirting with the female staff. Arthur Taber, also back at Issoudun looked on in disgust. "It is such a distasteful way in which to celebrate what might be called your 'deliverance from death' at the front," he wrote his mother on November 26. "I can't see why every educated man . . . shouldn't prefer to seek a church instead of a bar in which to express his feelings of gratitude."

Vaughn disagreed. On December 15, he was still languishing at Issoudun, still in the dark as to when he might return home. "Life is so slow around here that there is really not very much to write about," he told his parents. "The only pleasure we have is over at the Red Cross Hut, where it is quite comfortable, and there are some very nice girls, good meals, and a piano."

Vaughn closed his letter with a P.S—"Perhaps home by New Years yet!"

But he wasn't. He ate his Christmas dinner in the Red Cross Hut—the women dolling out cigarettes and candy to the officers—and spent New Year's Eve also at Issoudun. On January 12, he was in Angers, approximately 190 miles south-west of Paris, en route to the Atlantic port of Nantes. He was with Reed Landis, and in a quick letter to his parents he wrote, "I don't think we will have to wait long there. All the waiting is done."

George Vaughn and Reed Landis reached New York on February 3, 1919, on board the USS *Agamemnon*. Formerly the *Kaiser Wilhelm II*, a German passenger steamer completed in the spring of 1903, the *Agamemnon* began bringing American service personnel home from France in December 1918. In nine months she made nine voyages, ferrying nearly forty-two thousand soldiers and airmen back to the States.

Three days earlier America's "Ace of Aces," Eddie Rickenbacker, had arrived home to a tumultuous reception. All of his credited twenty-six victories had been achieved with the 94th Aero Squadron, the "Hat-in-the-Ring" boys, an American unit in the American air force. Thousands cheered Rickenbacker as he strolled down the gangplank of the White Star liner *Adriatic*; he was the all-American hero, whose portrait had adorned scores of newspapers a fortnight earlier when the War Department released the names of sixty-three American aces. All deserved credit but Rickenbacker was the "Ace of Aces."

Rickenbacker was whisked off to New York's Waldorf-Astoria where he was the guest of honor at a dinner hosted by the Automobile Association of America. Newton Baker, secretary of war, was the

Eddie Rickenbacker, America's "aces of aces," achieved twenty-six victories with the 94th Aero Squadron.

Painted on this fuselage is a knight on his charger chasing the devil, the insignia of the 91st Squadron.

guest speaker, and privileged he was, too, to shake the hand of America's most famous airman.

There was a small crowd waiting for the *Agamemnon*, including a reporter from the *New York Tribune*. Word had got out that the son of Judge Kenesaw Landis was on board, "second only to Captain Eddie Rickenbacker with a score of twelve." The paper mentioned in passing that Vaughn had shot down ten enemy aircraft—in fact he had thirteen victories—but the reporter was really interested only in Landis. Unfortunately "it was difficult to make him talk," the reporter told his readers the next day. "When asked if he were not one of our foremost pilots, he said he had not done any more than twenty or thirty other fellows, and only did what he was trained and paid to do."

Landis eventually fed the journalist a few tidbits about dogfights and narrow escapes. Vaughn took his chance and slipped away without saying a word. He had spotted his parents; he had come home.

Arthur Taber was still in France in February. On the second day of the month he wrote his parents from the American base at Orly airfield, a few miles south of Paris. He continued to ferry aircraft hither and thither, although he admitted that "it seems strange indeed to be still writing from France with hostilities ended and everyone bending every effort to get home; it seems as if one should at least be on the water, if not already at home."

On February 11, Taber took an aircraft for a test flight around Paris. Shortly after taking off from Orly the machine crashed to the ground. Taber "was killed instantly and suffered no pain."

Taber's death was listed in the *Washington Times* on March 5, 1919, one of 340 servicemen to have died in recent weeks from illness or accident. The paper noted that the latest figures raised to 271, 462 the number of casualties suffered by the United States in the War to end all Wars.

Arthur Taber is buried in the Suresnes American Cemetery on the outskirts of Paris. *Gavin Mortimer*

All You Had to Do Was Fly the Plane

It wasn't just Capt. Eddie Rickenbacker who returned from the war a hero. So did those Americans who served the French air force in the Lafayette Corps, subsequently immortalized in celluloid in the 1928 Hollywood film *The Legion of the Condemned*. That was also the year the French government unveiled the Lafayette Escadrille Memorial, just outside Paris, a towering tribute to the courage of the 265 American volunteers.

For the American airmen who had fought with the British there was no such fanfare. They were largely overlooked and ignored, perhaps victims of a popular press who questioned why any American would trek north to Canada and temporarily forfeit their nationality in order to fly with the British.

The oversight was still being perpetuated forty years later when, in his 1968 work *The Great Air War*, American author Aaron Norman did not acknowledge that as many as three hundred American pilots served in operational squadrons British during World War I, and from that total, twenty-eight aces between them shot down 294 enemy aircraft. Some of the responsibility for the lack of recognition accorded the Americans who flew in the RFC, and later the RAF, is attributable to the British policy of not glamorizing "aces" in the same way the French and the Germans did. The British believed more in the team ethos, that the whole of a squadron was greater than its individual parts.

The Lafayette Escadrille Memorial in Paris, inaugurated in 1928, honors the courage of those Americans who flew with the French air force. *Library of Congress*

One of the top aces of the war, Canadian Raymond Collishaw, credited with sixty victories and who later became an Air Vice-Marshal, wrote in his memoirs: "It always struck me as peculiar and rather unfair that the Americans who flew with the Lafayette Squadron should have received such great public acclaim whereas the many hundreds of Americans who flew as members of the British air forces, mostly with the RFC and the RAF, remain completely ignored."

The 94th Aero Squadron were known as the "Hat-in-the-Ring" boys because of the insignia painted on their aircraft's fuselages.

APPENDIX I

The Fate of the Few

Oliver "Bim" Bennett
Although he was one of the millions who contracted influenza in late 1918, Bennett recovered and slipped into obscurity, dying in 1963 at the age of sixty-eight. Shortly before his death Bennett was tracked down by the World War I aviation journal, *Cross & Cockade*. One of his clearest memories was reaching an altitude of 21,500 feet in his S.E.5a without oxygen. "I got a bit groggy," he recalled.

Billy Bishop
Bishop survived the war and was credited with seventy-two victories, although historians continue to question this total, suggesting the real number was far lower. Only von Richthofen with eighty victories and French ace René Fonck with seventy-five victories shot down more enemy aircraft in World War I. Bishop went into business between the wars, and was appointed director of the Royal Canadian Air Force in charge of recruitment upon the outbreak of World War II. He died in 1956 at the age of sixty-two.

Laurence Callahan
An investment banker after the war, Callahan maintained his friendship with Springs, and was his best man at his wedding in the 1920s. During World War II he returned to England, serving as an intelligence officer in the Eighth Air Force, although it was said he himself stopped flying after an inter-war accident nearly cost him his life. In the twilight of his life Callahan was happy to talk to historians about his wartime achievements, always with "a total lack of

pretense." Callahan died in 1977, the last of the Musketeers, and is buried in Louisville, Kentucky.

Frank Dixon
Officially credited with two victories, Dixon remained in the military and was the regional representative of the Material Command in Chicago, where he was discharged as a colonel in the U.S. Air Force after World War II. He retained close links to Princeton and in his later years was president of the Class of 1920. Dixon died at his California home in 1992, aged ninety-five.

John Donaldson
Something of a celebrity after his dramatic escape from German captivity, Donaldson was granted an audience with King George V at Windsor Castle upon his return to England. In 1919, he won the Mackay Gold Medal for coming first in the U.S. Army's transcontinental air race. Leaving the military the following year, Donaldson was appointed president of Newark Air Service Inc. in 1926. He continued to fly as a stunt performer, and was killed in an accident in September 1930.

John McGavock Grider
Grider's two sons, John and George, enjoyed distinguished naval careers in World War II; John died in 1984 aged seventy-four, George in 1991 aged seventy-nine.

For decades it was assumed Grider kept just one diary covering the period up to the Americans' arrival in England in early October 1917. This was the diary on which Elliott Springs said he based his 1927 book *War Birds: Diary of an Unknown Aviator*. When he was sued by the Grider family as a result of the book, Springs returned the diary. However, there was a second diary, covering the period October 3, 1917–February 7, 1918, that Springs never returned and which was found in his private papers after his death. However, in his book *Letters from a War Bird*, David Vaughan speculates that there was probably a third diary that ran from February 8. As evidence, Vaughan points to a letter Grider wrote to his friend Emma Cox, dated 27 February 1918, in which Grider states he's "keeping the service record up to date, fill[ing] it in every night and try[ing] to stay as near the truth as possible." No trace of this record has ever been found and Vaughan suspects Springs destroyed it "because it contained detailed references to Grider's social activities in London, and those descriptions might have been too vivid for family members to read."

Frank Hale

Hale finished the war with seven confirmed victories, remaining in the RAF until July 1919, when he returned to the United States. In November that year Hale was summoned to New York City to receive his DFC from the Prince of Wales on board HMS *Renown*. On the way to the port, Hale was involved in an automobile accident and had to postpone the ceremony for twenty-four hours. Subsequently, Hale settled in New York and led what was described as an "unconventional" life, one which included "periodic fights with the bottle."

America's entry into World War II gave him renewed purpose, and Hale enlisted in the Army Air Corps, despite a heart condition, only for the ailment to be discovered shortly after his arrival in England. Hale was shipped back to the States and was found dead at his home on June 7, 1944, the day after the invasion of France. "Quite possibly his old soldier's heart couldn't stand the thought of this tremendous battle going on without him," said a friend.

Lloyd Hamilton

Officially declared dead on October 12, 1918, Hamilton's body was eventually identified in the summer of 1919, and interred in an American military cemetery in France. In 1921, at his parents' request, he was exhumed and laid to rest in Pittsfield, Massachusetts. In 1932 the U.S. Army Air Corps dedicated a new airfield north of San Francisco in Lloyd Hamilton's honor, and the Hamilton Air Force Base remained active until the 1970s.

Reed Landis

Marrying Marion Keehn in 1919, Landis raised three children and also wrote his memoirs, *On the Roof of the War*, shortly after the war's end. He established an advertising business in Chicago, the Reed G. Landis Company, which also had an office in the Midwest. He served in the U.S. Army Air Force in World War II, reaching the rank of colonel, and died in in Arkansas in 1975, aged seventy-eight.

Jens Larson

In all, "Swede" was credited with nine victories, all flying S.E.5s with

84 Squadron. He returned to the States at the end of the war and enjoyed a successful career as an architect. He died in 1981, aged eighty-nine.

Oliver LeBoutillier

"Boots" finished the war an ace, though his exact number of victories ranges from six to eight, and embarked upon a colorful life post-war. After flying as a "barnstormer" back in the States, LeBoutillier went on to appear as a stunt pilot in eighteen Hollywood movies, including Howard Hughes's epic *Hell's Angels*. Hughes admired LeBoutillier's skills and he hired him as a test pilot. By the time LeBoutillier stopped flying he had flown some 19,000 hours. LeBoutillier settled in Las Vegas and became president of a pharmaceutical company. He died in May 1983, the last witness to the death of the Red Baron.

Fred Libby

For the rest of his life Libby suffered from his war injuries which, coupled with arthritis, left him "hunched over." Despite this he led a full and happy life, working in the oil industry for many years as a wildcatter. Later he founded Western Air Express, subsequently sold to Western Airlines, but he then lost most of his money drilling for oil. His granddaughter recalled that he took the setback with his customary sang-froid, saying: "True to his cowboy heritage, where a man's word and handshake were all there was and his honor was never to be forfeit, he lived with the consequences of his actions honorably and most admirably." Libby died in 1970, aged seventy-eight.

Donald Poler

Poler became a barnstormer in the 1920s, as a member of the Syracuse Aero Club, and hit the headlines in 1932 when he was part of an American Legion delegation receiving a $2,000 check for a high school aviation scholarship from film actress Marion Davies. He retired to Los Angeles, and died in September 1994, aged ninety-eight.

Orville Ralston

"Tubby" returned to Nebraska at the war's end, graduating from the state university as a doctor of dental surgery. Marrying a fellow dental student, Ralston was an active member of the Ainsworth community, serving as mayor and head of the local American Legion. Despite his settled life, Ralston joined the Army Air Corps in 1942 and was assigned to the 304th Bomb Group as an intelligence officer. In December that year he was killed when the B-17 he was travelling in crashed in Montana.

Bogart Rogers

Returning to the United States in May 1919, Rogers "borrowed a car and drove to Palo Alto where for the first time in almost two years, he and Isabelle were reunited." The pair married the following year and moved to Hollywood, where Rogers was employed by the *Los Angeles Examiner* flying photographers to important events. In the 1930s, Rogers enjoyed success as a screenwriter and novelist, and he also found time to invent a horse-race photo-finish camera. Rogers divorced Isabelle in the 1940s, and in 1950 married Frances Carrell. In 1961 he suffered a stroke, and five years later he died, aged sixty-nine. His letters to Isabelle were published by the Rogers family in 1996, entitled *A Yankee Ace in the RAF*. Isabelle died in 2000, aged 102.

Elliot White Springs

In 1921 Springs and Larry Callahan traveled to France to lay the ghosts of old friends to rest. On the ship across the Atlantic, Springs fell in love with Frances Ley, the daughter of a prosperous New York businessman. The pair were married a year later, and the union sparked a decade of feuding between Springs and his father. During that time Springs wrote *War Birds: Diary of an Unknown Aviator*, largely based on the diaries of John McGavock Grider. The book became a bestseller but provoked a row with Grider's sister, who threatened legal action if she wasn't given a share of the profits. Springs eventually paid out $12,500 in return for the right to use the diary, even though he always maintained that Grider had given him permission to quote from it in the event of his death.

Despite the dispute, Springs took an avuncular interest in the development of Grider's sons John and George, helping to fund their entry into the United States Naval Academy at Annapolis.

In 1931 Leroy Springs died, and his son finally felt ready to assume control of the family business, transforming Springs Mills from an ailing company into a phenomenally successful enterprise with assets of $138.5 million, compared to the $13 million it had when he took over from his father. Elliot Springs died of pancreatic cancer in 1959.

George Vaughn

On November 6, 1981, nine frail, gray men boarded a jumbo jet at John F. Kennedy Airport, New York, bound for Paris. They were going as the guests of François Mitterand, the French President, who had invited thirty World War I pilots to Paris for an event to mark the sixty-third anniversary of the conflict's end. Among the old men who slowly climbed the steps into the aircraft was George Vaughn who, as the *New York Times* noted, was eighty-four and a resident of Staten Island. The paper added that after destroying thirteen enemy aircraft, Vaughn had gone into engineering before forming his own company to build hangars. He also trained thirty thousand technicians for the Air Force during World War II.

Before boarding the aircraft to Paris Vaughn told the assembled reporters that back in his day, "all you had to do was fly the plane and shoot the guns." Mind you, he added as an afterthought, back in 1918 they didn't have wheelbrakes, or radios, or parachutes. The correspondent from the Associated Press asked Vaughn if he was apprehensive about meeting some of his former adversaries from the German air force. Not in the slightest, replied Vaughn. "You slap him on the back, buy him a drink and laugh about it."

George Vaughn died on July 31, 1989, aged ninety-two.

APPENDIX II

The Planes

The German Machines

Albatros D.I: Modelled on the French Nieuport 17, the D.I was introduced in 1916 and became a favorite of the German air force because of its rate of climb and diving speed. One notable innovation was that its fuselage was covered with plywood rather than stretched fabric, giving the machine greater strength.

Albatros D.II: A modification on the DI, the Albatros D.II made its first appearance over the Western Front in the fall of 1916 with the upper wings closer to the fuselage, on which were mounted two synchronous Spandau machine guns.

Albatros D.III: Introduced in January 1917, the D.III was an agile aircraft whose lower wing was reduced to allow pilots greater downward visibility. Nonetheless this was also a weakness, creating cracks in the lower wing during flight.

Pfalz D.III: A deadly menace to the RFC when introduced in the early summer of 1917, the Pfalz was impressively streamlined and a superb dogfighter with a far superior dive recovery to the Albatros D.III. This was because of its "tail plane with a flat top surface and a convex bottom," which automatically brought the Pfalz out of a dive.

Fokker D.VII: Described by George Vaughn as Germany's "greatest single-seater fighter," the D.VII made its first appearance in April 1918 and proved an instant success. A biplane of cantilever wing design with no external bracing, the machine had superb dive recovery and was reliable at high altitudes.

The Allied Machines

Sopwith Pup: Though the Pup—introduced in October 1916—was more agile and maneuverable than the Albatros at high altitudes, it had half the horsepower of its German rival and also carried just one .303 Vickers machine gun.

Sopwith Camel: Heralded as the superior version of the Sopwith Pup when it entered service in May 1917, the Camel's .303 Vickers machine guns' synchronization gear enabled them to fire through the propeller disc. But 90 percent of the Camel's weight was contained in the front seven feet of the aircraft making it less maneuverable than the Pup.

S.E.5: A single-seater biplane, the S.E.5 entered service in April 1917 and, with its 200-horsepower Wolseley Viper engine, proved itself fast and sturdy, if a little lacking in maneuverability. The machine had a Vickers that fired through the propeller and a Lewis on the top wing.

F.E.2b: A pusher aircraft (with the engine behind the pilot), the Farman Experimental 2 two-seater biplane was introduced in 1916 but was obsolescent the following year. The F.E.2b's observer stood in a nacelle in front of the pilot, contributing to its reputation as vulnerable to attacks from the rear.

Curtiss JN-4: Known as the "Jenny," the two-seater biplane never saw combat but was used as a training aircraft for North American cadets. Its reliability and maneuverability later saw it used as a barnstorming machine in the 1920s.

Avro 504: Recognizable by the skids between its wheels, the Avro was a tough aircraft that was designed in 1913 and used in the early part of the war for reconnaissance patrols and for bombing missions by the Royal Naval Air Service. It later became a favorite training aircraft of the RFC.

Bibliography

Books

Barker, Ralph. *The Royal Flying Corps in France: From Mons to the Somme*. London: Constable, 1994.

———. *The Royal Flying Corps in France: From Bloody April 1917 to Final Victory*. London: Constable, 1995

Bishop, Billy. *Winged Warfare*. London: Grosset & Dunlap, 1918.

Callender, Gordon W., ed. *War in an Open Cockpit: The Wartime Letters of Captain Alvin Callender*. West Roxbury, MA: WW1 Aero Publishers, 1978.

Clapp, Frederick Mortimer. *A History of the 17th Aero Squadron*. Garden City, NY: Country Life Press, 1920.

Clark, Alan. *Aces High: The War in the Air over the Western Front 1914–18*. New York: G. P. Putnam's Sons, 1973.

Franks, Norman. *American Aces of WWI*. Oxford: Osprey, 2001.

Franks, Norman and Frank Bailey. *Over the Front: A Complete Record of the Fighter Aces and Units of the United States and French Air Services, 1914–1918*. Havertown. PA: Casemate Publishers, 1992.

Hudson, James J. *In Clouds of Glory*. Fayetteville, AR: University of Arkansas Press, 1990.

Jones, H. A. *The Official History of the War in the Air*. London: Imperial War Museum, 1921.

Lambert, Bill, DFC. *Combat Report*. London: Corgi Books, 1975.

Libby, Frederick. *Horses Don't Fly*. New York: Arcade Publishing, 2000.

Morrow, John H. and Earl Rogers (edited by). *A Yankee Ace in the RAF: the World War I Letters of Bogart Rogers*. Lawrence, KS: University Press of Kansas, 1996.

Mortimer, Gavin. *Chasing Icarus: The Seventeen Days in 1910 That Forever Changed American Aviation*. New York: Walker, 2009.

———. *Fields of Glory: The Extraordinary Lives of 16 Warrior Sportsmen*. London: Andre Deutsch, 2001.

O'Brien, Lt. Pat. *Outwitting the Hun*. New York: Harper & Brothers, 1918.

Scott, A. J. *Sixty Squadron, RAF: A History*. London: Heinemann, 1920.

Springs, Elliott White. *War Birds: The Diary of an Unknown Aviator*. London: John Hamilton, 1927.

Sullivan, Alan. *Aviation in Canada, 1917–1918*. Toronto: Rous & Mann Ltd., 1919.

Stanwood, Arthur, ed. *The American Spirit; Letters of Briggs Kilburn Adams, lieutenant of the Royal Flying Corps*. Boston: Atlantic Monthly, 1920.

Taber, Sydney. *Arthur Richmond Taber* Privately printed, 1920.

Taylor, A. J. P. *The First World War*. London: Penguin, 2002.

Tichnor, Caroline, ed. *New England Aviators 1914–1918*. Boston: Houghton Mifflin, 1919.

Vaughan, David, ed. *Letters from a War Bird*. Columbia, SC: University of South Carolina Press, 2012.

Vaughn, George Jr. *War Flying in France*. Kansas: Military Affairs/ Aerospace Historian Publishing, 1980.

Whitehouse, Arch. *The Fledging*. London: Nicholas Vane, 1965.

Journals

Atlantic Monthly

Cross & Cockade

Nebraska History Journal

Over the Front

Video

William Madsen interviewing Oliver LeBoutillier at Nellis Air Force Base, 1976 (courtesy of the RAF Museum Hendon, London)

Newspapers

Boston Globe

Capital Times (Madison, Wisconsin)

Chester Times

Daily Mail (London, England)

Deming Headlight

Grand Rapids Tribune

Illinois Daily Free Press

Indiana Evening Gazette

New York Times

New-York Tribune

Oak Leaves (Oak Park, Illinois)

Rochester Weekly Republican

San Antonio Light

Sumner Gazette, Iowa

Sun (New York)

Syracuse Herald

Times (London, England)

Waterloo Times-Tribune
Washington Herald
Washington Post

Websites

AFamilyTree.net: Grider Family Tree
www.afamilytree.net/Griderprivacy/johnmcgavockgrider.htm

The Aerodrome—Aces and Aircraft of World War I
www.theaerodrome.com

Commonwealth War Graves Commission
www.cwgc.org

The Early Birds of Aviation
earlyaviators.com

Library of Congress: Chronicling America
chroniclingamerica.loc.gov

Oxford Dictionary of National Biography: Billie Carleton
www.oxforddnb.com/view/printable/64888

Index

Burden, Margaret Eaton, 69, 73
Butler, Charles, 103
Byng, Julian, 203

Callahan, Laurence, 25–26, *25*, 33, 40, 55–57, 59, 63–65, 69, 72–73, 87, 89, 93, *111*, 114–119, 143–145, 153–154, 182–188, 204–207, 215–216
Callender, Alvin, 120–124, *122*, 126–130, 134–136, 157, 159–162, 167, 190, 193–195, 197–199, 207, 213
Cambrai, France, 188, 192–195, 200
Campbell, Doug, *215*
Campbell, Jesse, 179
Campbell, Merton, 171–175, 177–178
Camp Borden, Toronto, 18–20
Canning, John, 118
Capelle, France, 150
Carleton, Billie, 89–95, *92*, 185
Carlton, Donald, 65
Carmania, 28–30, 32, 169
Carson, Harry, 162
Case, Lyman, 177
Caudron G.4, 77
Charlotte Observer, 205
Château-Thierry, France, 120
Clapp, Frederick Mortimer, 148–149, 170, 172–173, 175–176, 179, 200, 202
Clark, Dell, 61
Clay, Henry, 152, 153, *153*, 187–188, 205
Claydon, Arthur, 128, 134, 136–137
Clements, Bill, 152

Cochran, C. B., 90, 92
Collishaw, Raymond, 221
Conde, France, 212
Connersville Evening News, 17
Cooper bombs, 133–134, *133*, 175
Cox, Emma, 87, 89–90
Creech, Jesse, *145*, *169*, 169
Crystal Palace training facility (RNAS), 77
Cunningham, Jack, 170, 174–177
Curtis, Kent, *152*, 152
Curtiss Aeroplane Company, 21
Curtiss JN-4, 14, 21–22, 41, 45, 66

Davis, Mike, 99
Dawe, James, 131
Deetjen, William, 40
DeGarmo, Lindley, 65, 69
de Havilland. *See* Airco
Denton, H. B., 150
Department of Militia and Defense (Canada), 18
Deseronto, Canada, 122–123
de Veulle, Reggie, 91–93
Dietz, Philip, 40
Dirigibles, 11–12
Distinguished Flying Cross (DFC), 177, 186, 189, 197, 200, 204, 205
Distinguished Service Cross (DSC), 83, 188, 189, 201, 205, 215
Dixon, Frank, 24, 88n16, 103–104, 171–172, 175–176, 179–180
Donaldson, John, *137*, 137, 160–161, 164–166, 212, 213
Donaldson, Thomas, 137

Dore, Alan, 52
Douai, France, 192
Douglas, William Sholto, 99, *100*, 102, 103, 107
Dover, England training facility (RNAS), 78
Drocourt-Queant line, 190, 194
Dunkirk, France, 112
Dunn, R. C., *50*
Dwyer, Geoffrey, 28, 152
Dymmand (pilot), *111*

Eckert, Sam, 99, 107, 170, 172, 175
Evans, Robley D., 12–13, *13*

F.E.2. *See* Royal Aircraft Factory F.E.2
Fairchild, Franklin, 151
Farman MF.11 Shorthorn, 57
Falvy, France, 160
Farman Experimental 2. *See* Royal Aircraft Factory F.E.2
Farnum, William, 52
Farquhar, Lieutenant, 198
Faverolles, France, 133
Fédération Aéronautique Internationale, 76
56th Training Depot Station, London Colney, 59–61
The Flyer's Guide (Gill), 77
"Flying Circus." *See* German military, *Jagdgeschwader* I
Flynn, Jerry, 127, 162, 166–167, 190
Foch, Ferdinand, 155, 193
Fokker D.VII, 86, 134, 137, 152, 174, 176, 183